CRYSTAL ALCHEMY

*Manifesting Love, Magic, Spirit & Abundance
Using the Powers of Gemstones*

Lani Sharp

Photographs by Travis Wilcox

Copyright © 2019

All rights reserved. This book or any portion thereof may not be reproduced or used in any manner whatsoever without the express written permission of the author except for the use of brief quotations in a book review.

Printed in Australia
First Printing, 2018
ISBN: 978-0-6484641-5-0

White Light Publishing House
Melton, VIC, Australia 3337
whitelightpublishing.com.au

✭ ✭ ✭

*Dedicated to the Universe,
Creator of the entire mineral kingdom.*

✭ ✭ ✭

Beautiful and strong is the material of stones, but more beautiful and much more powerful is the mystery that emanates from them.

Chinese Poet & Alchemist, Li Po, 8th Century A.D.

CONTENTS

COVER STORY	9
INTRODUCTION	11
MY PERSONAL JOURNEY	13
CRYSTALS & ETHICS	16
CHAPTER 1 ★ ALL ABOUT CRYSTALS	**19**
CRYSTALS ★ THE PHYSICS & FORMATION	21
CRYSTALS & LUSTRE	23
CRYSTALS & HARDNESS ★ THE MOHS SCALE	23
CRYSTAL LIGHT & COLOUR EFFECTS	25
CRYSTALS, MAGIC & METAPHYSICS	27
CRYSTALS & COLOURS	33
CRYSTALLOMANCY ★ SCRYING ~ DIVINATION BY CRYSTAL	39
CRYSTALS ON AN ENERGETIC LEVEL	41
CRYSTAL CLEANSING	42
CHAPTER 2 ★ CLEAR QUARTZ ~ THE MASTER CRYSTAL	**49**
CHAPTER 3 ★ CRYSTALS & ASTROLOGY	**57**
CRYSTALS & THE PLANETS	59
CRYSTALS & THE MONTHS	62
CRYSTALS & THE SEASONS	63
CRYSTAL RELATIONSHIPS	70
CRYSTALS & THE ELEMENTS	72
CHAPTER 4 ★ CRYSTALS & THE CHAKRAS	**75**
THE CHAKRAS & ZODIAC CORRESPONDENCES	81
AURAS, CHAKRAS & CRYSTALS: A UNITED RELATIONSHIP	92
CHAPTER 5 ★ CRYSTALS & THEIR MEANINGS	**95**
FINAL WORD	221

COVER STORY

Choosing a cover for a book is rarely easy, but always exquisitely exciting! Indeed, I find it *the* most fun part of the literary creation process. The cover of any book is arguably its most important component, albeit at a superficial level; after all, it is what first and foremost draws a reader in, compels them to pick it up and open its pages to find out more. A cover should be compelling, thought-provoking, intriguing, eye-catching, inspiring, and above all, meaningful - meaning is what lends it its greatest power.

The reason I chose this particular photo, is because of its implied meaning. To me the cover image perfectly encapsulates the inherent message of this book. This image is especially potent because it contains the vast beauty and power of the five elements: Fire (lightning and electricity), Earth (crystals and sand), Air (storm and sky), Water (ocean and clouds), and Spirit (All intricately combined as One). This is what pure magic and alchemical transformation - a.k.a. the Philosopher's Stone that resides deep within the human spirit - are all intrinsically about. These reasons are also why I chose the title *Crystal Alchemy*; after all, the name of a book is its second most vital component.

It is my earnest wish that all readers of this book be somehow captivated, moved, and experience profound inner metamorphoses through learning about the wondrous, miraculous, and infinite powers of the gemstones described ... or even just one crystal that speaks to your very soul.

Magical blessings to all,

Lani

INTRODUCTION

All life is sacred, all created matter is created in accord with the laws of Light and seeded within all matter is the expression of the creator ... Crystals and gemstones are used as a vehicle because they are focal energy points of the Earth, and yet they are aligned to the heavens. They are the bridge between matter and spirit. They exist to remind us of our own brilliance, our own radiance, our own inner light, and our own inner knowing.

Miriam Kaplan

Shamans, witches, wizards, alchemists, magicians, and spiritual workers have known the powers of gemstones and crystals for hundreds of years. Propelled and accompanied by one's own mind force, crystals hold the capacity to change attitudes, to calm, to heal, to stimulate, to increase psychic abilities, and to manifest true, pure, *unadulterated magic* in our lives.

The alchemists of ancient times were often considered the precursors of modern chemists, but they were much more than that. Alchemy was not only a science of initiates, but also an all-encompassing philosophical movement, where the overt, material aim of discovering the Philosopher's Stone, which turned base metals into gold, often masked the loftier spiritual goal of refining the soul. The overt objective of alchemy was to turn any base mineral into gold, but there was also the esoteric aim of raising the base material of the human condition to the incorruptible 'gold' of the enlightened spirit, into a more religious, exalted, connected, and magical form. Some believed it had the power to prolong life and even promote immortality.

Over time alchemical practices became more sophisticated, taking on the magical, hermetic dimensions that we now see as one of its principal characteristics. Taking on a more spiritual angle, it acquired the grandiose title of *Ars Magna*, the 'Great Work'.

Crystals and gemstones have been used since antiquity, and alongside alchemical practices, to heal, to help expand awareness, to protect, to generate energy, for prophecy, for sealing, and for beauty. Crystals have always been our helpers, and it is on many levels and in many ways that they work; some of these are known to us now, others will be discovered in the future.

Spiritual author and shamanic expert Nevill Drury offered a compelling definition of a crystal as "A mystical symbol of the spirit. Its associations derive from the fact that crystal, though solid & tangible, is also transparent. Among many shamanic groups, natural crystals are regarded as power objects."

If you are truly open to crystal alchemy, teachings exist there, and knowledge will be revealed, for when you work with minerals and gemstones, you learn that there is a beautiful language to the stones. As you allow yourself to just *be*, crystals can speak to you, reflecting your own inner planes of awareness, as well as the outer and higher spheres and dimensions of Love and Light. The language of crystals will teach you that there is nothing to hold on to, for everything is in flux and ever-evolving. You can only perceive the lessons that they reflect as you live and walk your own true Path each and every day.

MY PERSONAL JOURNEY

Nothing is solid. There are no actual building blocks of the universe or matter, just streams of information and energy we classify as elements. Humans don't so much stand on the web of life as surf it.

Paul Hougham

I have always been a believer in all things spiritual, unseen, hidden and unexplained, holding fast to the 'rule' that states that just because something cannot be measured by science or other conventional tools and methods, that it does not exist. We have indeed been told by quantum physicists for millennia that everything, from your body to a flower in your garden, has a vibrational frequency and is made up of energy. Einstein furthered this by asserting that energy cannot be created or destroyed. So in effect, everything that exists, has always existed in some form or another, and it can never be destroyed, just transformed into a different form of energy. But it is still energy.

I learned this wondrous lesson for myself in an enchanting place just outside of Byron Bay, on the East Coast of Australia, one day when I was in my early twenties. I was footloose and fancy free, solo and free-spirited, on the road trip of a lifetime. One day, I awoke in my rainforest accommodation, and walked outside to the sound of tropical birdlife twirping, the hum of breakfast floating through the thick humid air, the smell of fresh rain-soaked soil, and the gentle voice of a young male. "We're heading off on a little day tour into the hills, bus leaving soon!" he called out, handing me an information flyer. As soon as I eyed the words 'Crystal Castle', I was sold on the whimsical idea. Shortly after, twelve of us climbed into the waiting mini bus, which was adorned with colourful flowers and painted with rainbows, swirls and the words, "Let it Grow!" Off we drove into the misty, thick-as-soup air, through winding roads and rolling hills. Although the tour was to cover other such exciting places and features such as the hippie town of Nimbin, a local market, and a tea stop at a unique little café, I was most looking forward to visiting this mysterious Crystal Castle, a palace of gemstones. I barely knew anything about crystals, but still had a fascination for these precious and semi-precious * little treasures of the Earth.

The Crystal Castle, and the amazing breakthrough I experienced there, did *not* disappoint! Located in the captivating Shambhala Gardens in the quirky town of Mullumbimby, we pulled into the driveway and walked to the entrance, captivated by the beautiful gems and related features surrounding this majestic place.

Inside, we explored the vast wares for a while, before being asked by a special character who worked in the shop to stand in a circle and close our eyes, with arms outstretched, palms upward. The twelve of us did as we were asked and stood in nervous but excited anticipation. He would walk around the circle, he told us, with a clear quartz crystal point, and do one of two things to each of our cupped hands: he would either wave the crystal point over our palms, or wave nothing at all but his fingers - afterwards, we would tell him what we thought had happened: had he used the crystal, or just his fingers? There was only one rule of the exercise: we had to absolutely keep our eyes closed tight the whole time. As he made his way around the circle, there were giggles and snorts for a time, then silence, as each person became transfixed by this man's amazing wordless 'experiment'.

Upon opening our eyes, he asked which one of us had 'felt' the crystal's powers. Only three people answered in the affirmative; I was one of them! What happened as he walked around the circle was incredible. The three people who gave the answer that yes, they had felt the crystal's energies, were the only three people over whose hands he had waved the clear quartz. The other nine people, over whose hands he hadn't waved anything, just his bare fingers, reported that they had felt nothing in particular - and they were right!

During the experiment, when he reached me, my eyes were shut tightly. I couldn't believe my sensations! I could feel a warmth, a gush of hot, gentle air, tracing an invisible circle around my palms. I could literally feel the circle as it was being 'drawn'. Then I felt a gentle tingle and a warm feeling of pressure, then a finally a lifting of the pressure, as he moved onto the next person. I had never experienced anything like it. From that moment onwards, I believed in the vibrational power of crystals, and I have never looked back!

One thing that really stuck out for me about this life-changing event, was that afterwards, aside from asking us if we had felt the crystal or not, the man offered no further words, no explanation for the phenomenon that had just occurred. He just smiled in gentle and genuine appreciation of our visit and participation and shuffled away. The reason, I realised later, he didn't use any words to explain the concept of crystal vibration, is because he *didn't need to* - for the message was oh so silent, but so deafeningly loud.

* Gemstones are generally divided into two classes – 'precious' and 'semi-precious'. Stones classified as precious are necessarily very rare but they must also possess the other important qualities of beauty and durability. Diamond, ruby, sapphire, emerald and black opal are always in demand and fine specimens demand high prices.

CRYSTALS & ETHICS

Knowing the lineage of a crystal is somewhat akin to knowing where the meat you're eating came from.

Colleen McCann

Before we delve into the glistening depths of the glorious mineral kingdom, I'd like to first bring up some karmic and ethical issues surrounding the mining, cultivation, farming, harvesting, extraction, production, and trade of the many millions of gemstones that flood the commercial market around the globe daily.

Over the many years of my journeys into the crystal realm, it has been brought to my awareness time and again how some industries, companies and cultures, whether motivated by greed, conflict, unrest, war, politics, profit, power, fairness, equality, or the inconvenient fact that their very livelihoods depend on it, will go to great - and disturbingly unethical - lengths to bring our gems to the table. The 2006 movie *Blood Diamond* highlighted some of the issues of that arise from the morally-unsound precious stone trade, and the plight and atrocities experienced by many that ensued.

This deeply-affecting movie features only a few of many aspects of the questionable ethics surrounding the production and sale of crystals, gems and minerals around the world. Indeed, the age-old systems for trading in stones and gems are often shrouded in mystery, corruption, exploitation and secrecy.

Many gemstones are extracted by large-scale industrial mines owned by companies with poor environmental records and a history of labour abuses and violations. Huge areas of land can often be excavated and effectively destroyed in the search and extraction of crystals. Many companies generate vast amounts of contaminants, toxins and other such seepages as by-products of their activity, which causes further destruction and degradation of our precious Earth. More still hold little regard for the fragility of the land: finite resources are whittled away until they are completely ravaged and spent, with no chance to renew, regenerate, and repopulate.

The sacredness of human life can also take a back seat in the quest to source gemstones. Many mines and sites, particularly in less-regulated Third World countries, are dangerous and hold little regard for safety or ethical standards of pay. In short, many people die or at the very least put their lives on the line in the sourcing of crystals that we take for granted and use for 'healing purposes'.

Pearls and coral are two materials that potentially have shady origins; pearls are often intensively farmed, and the extraction of coral for commercial purposes can detrimentally impact the marine ecosystem's delicate balance. For many the production, cultivation and harvesting of pearls may be considered a moral issue, for as many as 50 per cent of pearl oysters die in the process of being suspended in ocean cages for pearl-production. If you are concerned about the moral side of pearl farming, it would be wise to know where you are sourcing your gems from, and their ethical standards and practices. Similarly, coral can have dubious and less than transparent cultivation methods. When sourcing your coral, bear in mind that coral reefs are among the world's most vital yet fragile ecosystems, and materials taken from them should only be purchased from a reputable, ethical, and sustainable marine operator.

While it is not always possible to know where your gemstones are sourced from, asking questions and choosing to buy ethically and locally-extracted crystals about which you have some level of access to knowledge around origin and the methods used, is a fantastic start.

I have personally found that most sellers will try their best to be helpful and forthcoming in providing such information around the gemstones they sell. But the reality is that a great many do not really know where their gemstones originate from, much less the ethical standards used to bring them to you. This is understandable and to be expected; my suggestion is that in these situations, use your powers of discernment and intuition to decide whether or not buying a particular gemstone will upset your own delicate karmic balance.

CHAPTER ONE
★
ALL ABOUT CRYSTALS

CRYSTALS ✶ THE PHYSICS & FORMATION

Minerals * are naturally occurring chemical substances that make up rock and stone. They are inorganic substances, that have not been formed by a living process, such as that which creates the wood of trees. Minerals are composed of one or more of the ninety-odd natural elements in the Earth's crust, and the atoms of these elements slot together in particular ways to produce geometrical shapes called crystals. It is these crystal structures that make it possible for us to differentiate one mineral from another. Most minerals are chemical compounds, although some occur in a pure form such as gold. These pure forms are known as native substances. Some minerals share the same chemical compositions but are different minerals because their crystalline process varied from one another. For example, graphite and diamond are both forms of carbon, but the atoms comprising their crystalline structure are arranged differently due to the amount of pressure and temperature exerted upon them when they were forming.

The crystals found in the silicate mineral class are perhaps the most well-known and widely used crystals in our modern lives. The most common of these is the clear quartz crystal, which in its pure form is totally clear. Silicates are minerals that contain silica and oxygen in combination with other minerals or in a pure state as free silica (pure quartz is free silica). Of every 100 atoms in the crust of the Earth, more than 60 are oxygen, over 20 silicon, and around seven are aluminium. The silicates make up 25 per cent of the known minerals and nearly 40 per cent of the common ones. With a few exceptions all the igneous rock-forming minerals are silicates, thereby constituting well over 90 per cent of the Earth's crust.

The soil in and from which our food is grown and drawn is made up in large part of silicates, and it is found in all animal and vegetable tissues. Silicon is known as the 'magnetic element' because of its powerful electrical charge that is always ready to combine it with other elements. In modern industry silicon is found in its crystalline form of pure or clear quartz, being used in all facets of image and message transmission. Because of its transparency in both the infrared and ultraviolet portions of the spectrum and its ability to rotate the plane of polarisation of light, quartz is made into lenses and prisms for optical instruments. It is because of quartz crystals' ability to receive and transmit frequencies that it has made satellite, telephone, television, computer, and radio communications possible.

The three special qualities which give value to a gemstone are *beauty*, *durability* and *rarity*:

Beauty ★ Beauty is determined by a stone's depth of transparent colour (ruby or emerald), its colour alone (turquoise), or its property of splitting white light into spectral colours (zircon or diamond).

Durability ★ Durability depends on the degree of hardness, is a desirable quality of a gemstone. When used to embellish objects of personal decoration, particularly rings, a stone should obviously be hard enough to resist any abrasive or chemical agent which is likely to destroy its shine and mar its lustre.

Rarity ★ Rarity is often of the most importance, regarded above and beyond beauty or durability when judging the value of a mineral as a gemstone. A mineral may be fairly common, but fine pieces, suitable for cutting and polishing, may be very rare. A flawless stone of emerald is exceptionally rare, but when found it may well command a higher price than a diamond of comparable size and quality. Many other stones which undeniably possess qualities of beauty and strength are of significantly less value simply because they are less rare.

All gemstones - except coral, amber, jet, pearl and opal - are actually 'crystals' because they are formed from a crystalline structure. The six crystalline systems that distinguish gemstones are: Cubic (Isometric), Hexagonal, Tetragonal, Orthorhombic, Triclinic, and Monoclinic.

* A mineral can be defined as a substance having a definite chemical composition and atomic structure and formed by inorganic processes of nature. Virtually all gems are minerals and the properties possessed by a given mineral, which distinguish it from other minerals depend on two factors: *chemical composition* (the kinds of atoms from which it is built), and *atomic structure* (the spatial arrangement of the atoms).

ROCK FORMATION

The most common rock formations from which crystals spring, are:

Ingenous Rocks ★ Ingenous rock is formed through the cooling and solidification of lava or magma. This type of rock may form with or without crystallisation, either below the surface as 'intrusive' (plutonic) rocks, or on the surface as 'extrusive' (volcanic) rocks. The melting of pre-existing rocks in the Earth's mantle or crust, is caused by one or more of three processes: an increase in temperature, a decrease in pressure, or a change in composition. Most igneous rocks have formed beneath the surface of the Earth's crust.

Sedimentary Rocks ★ Sedimentary rocks are formed by the deposition of material at the Earth's surface and within bodies of water, the sediment being formed by weathering and erosion then transported to the place of deposition by water, ice, wind, mass movement or glaciers. Processes that cause mineral and/or organic particles to settle and accumulate, or minerals to precipitate from a solution, are collectively called sedimentation (particles that form a sedimentary rock by accumulating are called sediment).

Metamorphic Rocks ★ Metamorphic rocks arise from the transformation of existing rock types, in a process known as metamorphism. When the original rock is subjected to heat (temperatures greater than 150 to 200 degrees Celsius and pressure (1,500 bars), it results in profound physical and/or chemical change in the rock. Sometimes they are formed simply by being so deep beneath the Earth's surface that they are subjected to the great pressure of the rock layers above, as well as high temperatures. They can also form from tectonic processes such as continental shifts / collisions, which cause friction, pressure and distortion.

CRYSTALS & LUSTRE

Lustre is the quality of light reflected from the surface of a mineral and is a valuable aid to its identification. The types of lustre are:

Metallic ★ Has the appearance of metal (usually shiny), e.g. pyrite
Adamantine ★ Appears hard, sparkling and/or brilliant, e.g. diamond
Vitreous ★ Glassy, e.g. quartz
Resinous ★ Has a texture like resin, e.g. amber
Waxy ★ Has a texture and appearance like wax, e.g. turquoise
Pearly ★ Iridescent and sometimes rainbow or shiny tints, e.g. muscovite
Greasy ★ Appears to be covered with a thin film of oil or polish, e.g. opal
Silky ★ Appears to be made of silk threads, e.g. selenite
Dull or Earthy ★ Minerals which have little or no lustre, e.g. clay

CRYSTALS & HARDNESS ★ THE MOHS SCALE

Hardness describes how easily a crystal can be scratched. In 1812, a German mineralogist, Friedrich Mohs, chose 10 well-known minerals and arranged them in order of their 'scratch hardness' to serve as standards of comparison, and this 'Mohs' scale still forms the universally accepted standard. Minerals which are categorised with a high number on the Mohs scale will scratch those rated at a lower number. This scale starts at hardness 1 for Talc, and ends at hardness 10, which is diamond. Crystals which a hardness of less than 5 tend to cleanse emotional imbalances by absorbing them.

Substance	Hardness *
Talc	1
Amber, Gypsum	2
Calcite, Jet	3
Fluorite, Malachite, Pearl	4
Apatite, Lapis Lazuli, Obsidian, Opal, Turquoise	5
Agate, Carnelian, Garnet, Jasper, Hematite, Jade	6
Felspar, Jasper, Labradorite, Moonstone, Pyrite	6
Onyx, Peridot, Quartz, Tiger's Eye, Tourmaline	7
Emerald, Topaz	8
Ruby, Sapphire	9
Diamond	10

* This scale is not proportional; for example, diamond is 120 times harder than ruby (9), but 4 million times harder than talc (1)

Hardness is the ability of a mineral to resist abrasion, and the following gives some idea as to this quality at each level of hardness:

1 ★ Easily scratched by a fingernail.
2 ★ Scratched with difficulty by a fingernail. Will not scratch a copper coin.
3 ★ Not scratched by a fingernail. Scratches copper and is scratched by copper.
4 ★ Does not scratch glass. Scratches copper.
5 ★ Scratches glass with difficulty and is scratched by glass with difficulty.
6 ★ Scratches glass easily. Scratched with difficulty by a knife blade.
7 ★ Not scratched by a knife blade. Scratched with difficulty by a file.
8 ★ Will scratch quartz but not corundum. Is scratched by corundum.
9 ★ Will not scratch diamond. Will scratch all those on lower levels of hardness.
10 ★ Not scratched by any known natural substance. Will scratch any other natural substance.

CRYSTAL LIGHT & COLOUR EFFECTS

Many crystals show striated light effects or colour effects which do not relate to their body-colour and are not caused by their chemical composition or impurities. These effects, which are caused by reflection, refraction, and interference, can make a gemstone appear even more mystical, unique and magical.

Adularescence ★ Interference phenomena of the layered structure are the cause of this effect, where an opalescence or 'billowy light' glides over the surface when the stone is cut en cabochon *. An example of adularescence is moonstone.

Asterism ★ This is the effect of light rays forming a star (Latin *aster*, meaning star). Ruby and sapphire cabonchons can show effective six-rayed stars. There are also four-rayed stars and, rarely, twelve-rayed stars. It is usually created through reflection of light by thin fibrous or needle-like inclusions that lie in various directions within the stone. Asterism can also occur in synthetic, or mad-made gems.

Aventurescence ★ This is the colourful play of glittering reflections of small plate or leaf-like inclusions. An example of this effect is green aventurine quartz, which can contain fuschite or hematite inclusions.

Chatoyancy ★ Meaning cat's eye effect (French *chat*, meaning cat), this is an effect which resembles the slit eye of a chat and is caused by the reflections of light by parallel fibres, needles or channels. This phenomenon is most effective when the stone is cur en cabonchon in such a way that the base is parallel to the fibres. When the stone is rotated, the so-called cat's eye glides over the surface. The effect is known in cat's eye, hawk's eye, tiger's eye and bull's eye, among others.

Iridescence ★ The rainbow-like hues (Latin *iris*, meaning rainbow) seen in some crystals is caused by cracks or structural layers breaking up light into spectral colours. Fire agate is an example of this phenomenon.

Labradorescence ★ Iridescence in metallic hues, found especially in labradorite (hence the name) and spectrolite. Blue and green effects are most commonly found, but the whole spectrum is often observed.

Opalescence ★ This is the milky-blue or pearly appearance of common opal, and is created by reflection of short wave, predominantly blue, light. It should not be confused with play-of-colour.

Orient ★ The iridescence in pearls, which is created through diffraction and interference of the light by the shingle-like layers of aragonite platelets near the surface of the gem.

Play-on-colour ★ This is the effect of flashes of rainbow colours in opal which change with the angle of observation.

Silk ★ Reflection of fibrous inclusions or canals that cause a silk-like appearance, which is an effect especially desirable in rubies and sapphires. If the needles are sufficiently numerous, the gem can display chatoyancy if cut en cabonchon.

Luminescence ★ Luminescence (Latin *lumen*, meaning light) is a collective term for the emission of visible light under the influence of certain rays, as well as by some chemical or physical reactions, but not including pure heat radiation. The most significant of these phenomena for the testing of gems is the luminescence under ultraviolet light, which is called fluorescence ^. When the substance continues to emit light after irradiation has ceased, the effect is called phosphorescence (named after the light property of phosphorus).

* Polished but not faceted

^ The name 'fluorescence' is derived from the mineral fluorite, which is the substance in which this light phenomenon was originally observed.

Gems owe their origins to the stars.

Plato

CRYSTALS, MAGIC & METAPHYSICS

Each crystal and mineral of the earth embodies different qualities, patterns or potential expressions of the Divine language, the silent whispers of the Universe. If we can accept the fact that the human body is a sophisticated, multi-faceted antenna system comprised of a crystalline matrix that is constantly transmitting and receiving all manner of energies, it could then be assumed that energy and body workers who use quartz, shells and stones, which are also crystalline materials, have the power to create resonant interactions with the liquid 'crystal' structures found in human tissues. It could even be said that we are all made of essentially the same substances and structures, and that crystals and gemstones vibrate at varying energetic levels which can connect with our own in order to 'buzz' and dance together to make a harmonious one-song both within and without.

The reason crystals have become so popular is that they fulfil an important need for human beings: they bridge the gap between science and magic. They are used in science and technology in the form of the silicon chip to receive, store and transmit information, in computers, radio, lasers, television, telecommunications, and so on. And crystals are used as a tool in healing, visualisation and meditation in exactly the same way - to receive, store and transmit energy.

During their formation, minerals undergo the process of 'crystallisation', during which a mineral that has been liquid at high temperatures cools and in doing so acquires a natural polyhendronic form and an internal structure which is characterised by the order in which its molecules are distributed. This internal structure is the reason that the electromagnetic energy of minerals resonates at a regular frequency which, in turn, gives them the properties which harmonise and balance the energy of other bodies. From this, we can safely say that the basic properties and the atomic organisation of the components of the gems and minerals determine their possible range of beneficial effects. According to much eastern wisdom, crystals emit vibrations of energy. Believers say that they can exert a positive effect on us and in short, improve the quality of our lives.

The closer such crystal formations lie to the magnetic core of the Earth, the greater their magnetic field. For example, all quartz mined in areas such as Arkansas in the United States - a region which is extremely close to that core - emit powerful electromagnetic energies, and this area has provided some of the purest quartz crystals known to humankind. Much of the output mined in this region has and is being used by the electrical industry to improve people's lifestyles and technology.

Many studies and experiments show that many crystals also respond to our 'thoughts'. When we project loving thoughts towards a quartz crystal, for example, the pure vibrations we emit are absorbed within the energy field of that crystal and, being a positive vibration, the response will be an almost instantaneous release of its electromagnetic energies.

All crystals work through vibrational balancing and by channelling energy. Much of the magic of crystals is in their colour, which is determined by the rate at which their atoms vibrate; these vibrations can be matched to the energy given by your own body's aura. And just as light can be focused and refracted through gemstones, so too can all kinds of psychic energy, from healing energies to Divine communications.

In *Stones of the New Consciousness*, author Robert Simmons states, "(Wearing stones) is the simplest self-healing practice you can do, yet it is among the most effective. Wearing or carrying stones whose vibrations correspond with the qualities you wish to embody brings their currents into engagement with the Liquid Crystal Body Matrix ... you may notice over time the phenomenon of energetic integration and may initially feel the currents of the stones very tangibly ... (over time) one's body and vibrational field internalise the stone's currents and adjust to them, making them a part of one's own vibrational make-up. (And) we know from the resonances we feel in the body that crystals emanate tangible, if immeasurable, currents."

Gemstones can help us attune to higher vibrations and bring them into our own experience and being. This theory of crystal resonance suggests that the characteristic energy patterns emanated by any stone can be transferred into the 'liquid crystal medium' of our bodies through resonance. Our bodies, being composed of these tuneable liquids, can mimic and mirror any consistent vibrational pattern with which we come into contact; we can therefore resonate with the healthful qualities of various crystals and minerals.

Crystals and precious stones have been valued throughout world cultures over many centuries for their healing virtues and capacities to imbue courage, strength, invulnerability, clairvoyance, love and numerous other qualities. Wearing gemstones is one of the simplest and most effective self-healing practices you can undertake and wearing or carrying those stones whose vibrations correspond with the qualities you wish to embody brings their energetic currents into engagement with your body.

Once we begin to understand the language of crystals, we can see how they can be used for manifestation purposes. The ability to manifest what we need in the physical plane through our own power of magnetism is possible if we become aligned with the underlying energy force that exists in the Universe. This alignment comes through inner attunement and can be greatly aided by crystals that are in harmony with our desires or intentions. Since crystals function as a bridge between the subtle and the physical bodies, by learning to work with crystals, you can even develop the ability to infuse the stones with your consciousness. Through gemstones, whatever you wish to have fulfilled in your life, can be manifested. Indeed, your consciousness can actually shape the magnetic energy field inherent in crystals according to your thoughts and intentions. For the purpose of manifestation, both pointed crystals that direct the flow of energy and crystals with 'windows' are powerful tools.

We need to pay attention to our thoughts also. A thought held in your imagination with focus and passion, backed by the force of your will, and fired by your emotion and desire, will become imprinted deeply on your subconscious mind and take form on these astral levels. With repeated visualisation (seeing with your mind's eye the end result, e.g. a new car, a great night out, travel to a new place, meeting your soul mate) it will gather energy and momentum and power until it eventually manifests on the physical plane. This is the creative process. Everything we create, without exception, begins first as a thought in the mind. The initial idea, or flash of inspiration, is received from the Universal Mind when it enters the arena of your conscious awareness. This desire or idea may remain as a wish, a whimsical notion, for a while. But when that thought-form is backed by firm willpower (the pressing intention to make it manifest), concentration, emotion and clear-cut visualisation of the end result, it must eventually gather energy and weight until its vibration becomes so dense and intense it *has* to manifest as a physical reality. Once you create a clear thought-form through visualisation, you instantaneously put into operation the Law of Attraction, a natural law which at its most basic level states that 'like attracts like'. Everything in creation is energy (even though it may appear solid) and the nature of energy is magnetic. Energy vibrating at a particular rate will magnetise to it things vibrating at a similar rate. So, once you have created and empowered a clear-cut thought form on the astral level, it will begin magnetising to it all the conditions and circumstances for it to manifest in physical form. Through the Law of Attraction, the vibration that you project or 'put out there' determines exactly what you will receive. This law is infallible, immutable and exact.

Ancient people have indicated that the rates of vibration in gems differ with the needs of the chemical entities composing them, and it may well be further assumed that life exists in a gem just as it does in another form in a plant or an animal. Colour, in essence, is vibration, and is crystallised in a crystal and such immense vibration defies the tangible perceptions of humans. A purple amethyst vibrates at the phenomenal rate of 750 trillion per second, whilst a red ruby vibrates at 460 trillion, making it scientifically possible to demonstrate distinct powers by the evidence of known vibratory action.

Crystals ultimately act as 'transmitters' and 'amplifiers' of your will or intentions - as long as your will or intentions are in sympathy with the crystal's energy. The mineral kingdom refers to stones, minerals and crystals and the associations and vibrations they carry. When working with stones, we are working with several different layers of spiritual energies, and although they can be regarded as inanimate 'psychic batteries', they are actually moving, vibrating masses of energy which transmit potential and power into our lives. Some crystals and stones even have receptive powers, which means they can absorb energy and retain it within until cleansed.

From antiquity to the present day, back even to the dawn of humanity and into the future, precious stones and talismans have been held in high esteem by people the world over, primarily because of their beauty, but also for the qualities ascribed to them on account of their virtues, as transmitters of good luck and to avert misfortune. The marked influence on the lives of whole cultures, civilisations and individuals, intensifies our interest in them, so it is little wonder that belief in the mysterious properties associated with crystals should have endured the many centuries beyond their initial 'discovery'.

The philosophers of thousands of years ago, understanding gemstones' suitability as mediums for the transmission of astral forces and vibrations, invested them with much importance, attributing to them spiritual as well as physical and material powers, special characteristics, and medicinal and curative qualities.

Although it is untrue that the only stones you can usefully wear are the ones astrologically matched with your Sun sign or ruling planet, those which align with your Sun sign or ruling planet are the most fortuitous and appropriate 'attractors' and 'amplifiers'.

Twelve oracular gemstones were described in the Bible, as the author of *Exodus* (28-15 and 17-21) knew them. Yahweh spoke to Moses about the breastplate he would have to wear to train for priesthood, and described it to him in these words: "And thou shalt make the breastplate of judgement with cunning work; ... And thou shalt set in it settings of stones, even four rows of stones; the first row shall be a sardius, a topaz, and a carbuncle. And the second row shall be an emerald, a sapphire and a diamond. And the third row an opal, an agate and an amethyst. And the fourth row a beryl, and an onyx, and a jasper; they shall be set in hold in their inclosings. And the stones shall be with the children ... (all) twelve (of them)."

The precious stones ascribed to the twelve months of the year were those worn in the breastplate of the High Priest, and it was believed that the Divine revelations obtained by the shining or dullness of the stones in the Urim and Thummim, due to some virtue inherent in them, were indicative as to whether the atonement had been accepted or not. These twelve stones, engraved with twelve anagrams of the name of God, had a mystic power over the zodiac, harmonising the twelve angels and good spirits who had affinity with the twelve tribes of Israel.

THE CLASSIFICATION OF THE BREASTPLATE

Hebrew Name of Stone	Modern Name of Stone	Sign of Zodiac
1. Odem	Red Hematite	Aries
2. Pitdah	Emerald	Taurus
3. Bareketh	Marble	Gemini
4. Nofek	Chrysoprase	Cancer
5. Shoham	Sardonyx	Leo
6. Jashpeh	Jasper	Virgo
7. Lesham	Opal	Libra
8. Shebo	Banded Agate	Scorpio
9. Achlamah	Amethyst	Sagittarius
10. Tharshish	Serpentine	Capricorn
11. Sapir	Lapis Lazuli	Aquarius
12. Yahalom	Clear Quartz	Pisces

Given that the 'compilers' of the Bible lived during a time when astrological belief was prevalent in Babylon, it seems valid to assert that these previously named gemstones would have some astrological basis. Further, since these ancient people supposedly made correlations between each of the twelve precious stones, and one of the twelve zodiac signs, there are seven crystalline systems set down in crystallography (or the science of the laws which influence the formation, structure and geometric, physical and chemical properties of crystallised matter) as analogous with the seven traditional ruling planets of the zodiac.

However, nobody is under the rule of one planet alone. We are all in essence a complex mixture of every planet, many elements and varying aspects, depending on their positions, placements and prominence in our birth chart. Everything that goes on in the skies above us affects what is going on here on Earth, and also *within* us. Your lucky stones are to assist you to tune into your Sun sign's energy and planetary influences, but you are by no means limited to the ones listed for your sign alone. Above all, let your stones, whichever ones you choose, work for you and allow them to transport your very own unique and magical energy into the wider Universe.

Wearing stones will affect your aura, according to the nature of the crystal *. The purchasing phase of acquiring a gemstone is just as important as the use of it thereafter. When buying a stone in person, buy the one that you are attracted to, avoiding if possible polished stones. If you are right-handed, hold it in your left hand, if it feels good to you, it is meant to be yours and it will work for your intents and purposes. The reason for this is that your dominant hand is your main transmitter of energy, and your secondary hand is your receiving hand.

So, if you are right-handed, your right hand is your dominant hand. If you hold a crystal in this dominant hand, you will tend to impress your feelings on it instead of *receiving* its energy.

Although Full Moon-cleansing is perhaps the most well-known method by which to purify stones, the Sun is just as effective, and exposing crystals and gems to sunlight is an excellent way to energise them.

The Native American Indians believe that each stone has its own spirit, therefore you can 'speak' to it and request it to help you in specific ways. For absolute maximum accuracy in directing the Force for your intents and purposes, use a crystal with a whole, intact point, not a broken point. Broken points give a scattered blast of energy, whereas energy from a whole point is akin to a laser beam in its intensity and focus.

You can carry more than one type of stone at a time; they do not cancel each other out. They can be carried in your pocket, a bra cup, a pouch fastened to clothing, or you can simply wear them as jewellery on many parts of the body. If you wish to absorb (attract, increase) energy, wear or carry the stone on your left side. If you want to transmit (send out) a vibration, wear or carry the stone on your right side.

CRYSTALS & COLOURS

(These meanings are commonly recognised; however the meanings may vary from culture to culture)

Violet / Purple: Magic, Mystery, Imagination, Transformation, Spirituality, Intuition
Indigo: Intuition, Higher Planes, Meditation, 'Seeing', Mental Healing
Blue: Peace, Spirituality, Healing, Calming, Restoration, Strengthening
Green: Healing, Nature, Fertility, Calmness, Balance, Serenity, Restoration
Yellow: Happiness, Joy, Memory, Communication, Confidence, Expression
Pink: Love, Comfort, Nurturance, Friendship, Forgiveness, Trust, Serenity
Orange: Vitality, Creativity, Confidence, Joy, Optimism, Attraction, Abundance
Red: Sexuality, Passion, Positivism, Drive, Courage, Desire, Vitality, Joy
Black: Grounding, Earth, Stability, Transformation, Protection, Absorbing, Banishing Negativity
Grey: Maturity, Security, Peace, Shielding from Psychic Attack, Neutralising
White: Protection, Purification, Clarity, Inspiration, Spiritual Strength, Wisdom
Brown: Earth, Orderliness, Stability, Security, Perseverance
Turquoise: Intuition, Idealism, Prosperity, Peace, Tonic
Multicoloured: Possibilities, Joy, Vision
Gold: Wisdom, Self-confidence, Protection, Ambition, Recovery, Resilience

Silver: Luck, Truth, Intuition, Feminine Spirituality, Attracting Love
Metallic: Alchemy, Wealth, Magic

This list is a guide to which colour crystal to use in order to draw in the required energy:

WHITE ★ Purifies the physical, emotional and etheric bodies. Originality, beginnings, clarity, inspiration, good health, spiritual development, contact with angels and spirit guides. The 'colour' of purity, inspiration and spiritual strength, white is the colour of inner peace and of the connection we have with the Universe. Relating to the Crown chakra, white crystals are used for the higher intellect, wisdom, soul, and spirit.

PINK ★ Love, self-respect, self-worth, reconciliation, happy relationships, kindness, restoring trust. Pink is the colour of love in all its forms. It is nurturing and comforting, calming and restful. Pink stones heal emotional imbalances and gently energise your system. The colour of universal love, pink benefits the heart and removes sorrows and past hurts. Restorative and softening, it inspires creativity and self-acceptance, and soothes in times of emotional pain.

RED ★ Energy, passion, sexual desire, positive change, determination, initiative, overcoming obstacles. Red activates the energies of the body and encourages vitality, courage and strength. Red and orange stones are warming and stimulating. The colour of fire, they can be used wherever a body system is sluggish or warmth is needed. Believed to promote fertility and connect us to our sexual energy, they can be used to awaken a depleted Base chakra. Awakening energy, joy and vibrancy, they can also inflame our emotions, and if anger or fear is present, they can be balanced with a soothing green, pink or blue stone.

ORANGE ★ Release from responsibility, creates a personal magnetic field, confidence. Orange stimulates and strengthens the nervous system, and promotes courage, joy, creativity, fertility, abundance, self-esteem, and optimism. Orange stones act as mental and creative energisers, stimulating personal power and drive. (See also under 'RED')

YELLOW ★ Mental awareness. Yellow stones reflect the energy of the Sun and promotes clarity, alertness, logic, memory, determination, tests, communication, money-making, conventional healing, and optimism. Warming, stimulating and mood-boosting, but not as 'hot' as red crystals. Yellow crystals inspire and motivate and fill us with purposeful energy, as well as stimulating the mental and nervous systems.

GREEN ★ Heals the heart, and is good for overall restoration, abundance, balance, fertility, love, commitment, growth, beauty, environment, healing via nature, and gradual increases of health, wealth and luck. Green and blue are the colours of new life, growth, calmness, regeneration and deep but gentle healing. They are cool, soothing, and work towards harmony. Many stones contain blue and green and their properties are therefore a blending of the two colours.

TURQUOISE ★ Intuition, idealism, prosperity, peace, tonic. Blue-green stones resonate with the subtle levels of being and open up our metaphysical abilities.

BLUE ★ Healing, protective, tonic, strengthening, restorative, and peaceful, blue has a calming effect and can be used to aid meditation, to enhance inner attunement, and also to relax and restore the nervous system. (See under 'GREEN')

PURPLE / VIOLET ★ The regal colour of transformation, purple and violet hues quicken vibrations and transmute what is negative into positive. Purple strengthens the nervous system and promotes elevation of the soul and spirit. Purple is good for imagination, dreams, psychic powers, intuition, teaching, counselling, healing from higher sources, and banishing past sorrows or present troublesome influences. The colour of spirituality and awareness, it is at once both uplifting and soothing.

INDIGO ★ Indigo has mystical and transformative properties and encourages mental healing and attunement.

GOLD ★ Wisdom, self-confidence, protection, fulfilling ambitions, large infusion of money or resources, recognition, longevity, recovery and resilience after setbacks, minor miracles, healing when prognosis is not good.

SILVER ★ Luck, unexpected money, truth, intuition, Lunar connections, feminine spirituality, attracting love, natural fertility cycles.

BROWN ★ Stability and Earth, grounding, practical matters, security, accumulation of money, property, perseverance, learning new skills in later years.

BLACK ★ Material world, protection, absorption. Black crystals powerfully connect us to the Earth, they steady us and help us maintain our centre, stabilising the emotions by deflecting negativity and dispelling fear and confusion. Black stones are protective, grounding, and awakening one to their subconscious mind. They are good for transformation, peaceful endings, grief, acceptance, blocking negative forces, psychic protection, and banishing sorrow, guilt and destructive influences.

GREY ★ Adaptability, peace-making, neutralising unfriendly energies, keeping secrets, shielding from psychic attack.

MIXED COLOURS ★ Coloured crystals are of particular benefit in crystal therapy because the combined shades are able to complement and enhance each other's powers and properties. This may occur for different reasons, such as the stone contains more than one mineral, it has been affected by different levels of heat to parts of it, it contains veins of other materials that have been affected by a chemical reaction, or it is found in the matrix of another stone (such as ruby in zoisite). Some two or more toned gems include: agate, ametrine (purple and golden yellow), chrysocolla (blue and green), kyanite (blue and white), fluorite (green and purple), malachite (green and black), rhodonite (pink and black), watermelon tourmaline (green and pink), snowflake obsidian (black and grey), and ukanite (green and pink). Crystals that combine two colours work on energies linked with those colours. If both colours work on the same energy, this enhances the overall effect.

METALLIC ★ Alchemy, wealth. The main crystals that fall into this unusual colour grouping are bornite (peacock ore), hematite, magnetite, marcasite (silver pyrites) and pyrites (fool's gold). This group of crystals were among the first to be used by cave-dwelling humans. Marcasite and pyrites were used as sources of sulphur, which is/was of great importance to alchemists. Being very Earthy with their high metal content, metallic crystals have often been used for magic associated with the Earth, such as attracting wealth. They were also associated with increased affluence because they were often found around deposits of gold and silver. Copper bracelets * are worn to ease the painful symptoms of arthritis, rheumatism, Carpel Tunnel syndrome, lumbago,

PMS, sciatica and other general aches and pains. Balancing the levels of copper in one's bodily system, they can assist with the production of red blood cells and the utilisation of vitamin C and protect one from the harmful effects of free radicals.

* Copper bracelets are often magnetised and should not be worn by people with pacemakers or pregnant women

CRYSTALLOMANCY ✴ SCRYING ~ DIVINATION BY CRYSTAL

Is it possible to read the future in a crystal ball? Yes, many clairvoyants, magicians, witches, alchemists, spiritual workers, and those who make use of this medium for deciphering the future or distant arcana of those who consult them, will reply. Otherwise known as scrying and sphereomancy, gazing into a crystal ball * to bring the future, present or past into focus has been practised for centuries and has always attracted immense curiosity, scepticism, and interest.

Various cultures and civilisations saw spirits in waters, springs, ponds, lakes, and ice. In fact, when early humans went near water, they would have seen the reflection of an ethereal, elusive being, who looked like themselves, which they may have thought to be doubly magical. But they also read in it 'signs' revealed by the movements of the water: waves, swirls, eddies, bubbles. The basic principles of divination by crystal merge, therefore, with the discovery of the natural mirror and the awareness of the double and the soul, which is found in the Greek legend of Psyche. Catoptromancy, or divination by mirror, was commonly practised by Greek magicians and soothsayers, who placed a mirror into the water of fountains or sacred springs to read omens from them. The appearance of what today we call the crystal ball is much more recent, dating from the middle of the 13th century, in medieval France.

Why did humans cut the crystal in the shape of a sphere? Quite simply because the sphere or ball, symbolically is associated with the circle, it represents absolute perfection, and it has no beginning or no end, revealing the world and Universe in its entirety. As for the crystal, it is the natural instrument which the 'gods' and Divine powers have gifted people so that those people can make contact with them, a sort of tool of communication between the visible and the invisible. So, in the beginning, these two symbols combine possessed a magic, sacred character, and a veritable ritual was organised around the use of the crystal sphere. The following important principles applied to the use of crystal balls: The sphere had to be of rock crystal (clear quartz) or beryl, perfectly pure and with no bubbles or marks in it; When it was not being used, the sphere had to be kept protected from the sunlight, which could destroy its magical powers and mar the purity of the crystal (allowing the moonlight to be reflected in it, however, was advisable); The crystal sphere had to be put on display in a secret place, in the north, at a constant, mild temperature - this place was known only to the crystal-gazer; The crystal-gazer would consult the sphere only at night, at the time of a Waxing or Full Moon, in the presence of a single inquirer, in the greatest secrecy, without ever touching the crystal.

Popularly associated with fortune-telling, as the crystal-gazer stares fixedly into a crystal or surface, they focus their gaze and enter a state of trance reverie. Paranormal visions may then arise, which form the basis of divination. The first impressions may be hazy or misty, but according to many credible accounts this effect gradually gives way to specific visionary scenes. Occultists believe that the crystal ball or surface is a focus for the medium's psychic perception, and therefore it does not, in itself, cause the visions to appear. As with many magical systems, techniques and rituals, it is of course, all in the eye and psychic receptivity of the beholder.

* Crystal spheres aren't the only object used for scrying. Some magical practitioners use a bowl of water, a glass of wine, polished surfaces of any material, polished metal, a faceted jewel, and even an ordinary mirror and other reflective surfaces.

People love stones, and apparently stones love people. Like the angels they may be, they seem endlessly willing to serve the wellbeing of humans and to help us achieve our desires ... Unlike people of the ancient past, we now have access to virtually the entire mineral kingdom. We have the opportunity to work like modern alchemists, combining and arranging the stones and their currents, looking for combinations and patterns that can help us enhance our inner and outer lives.

Robert Simmons

CRYSTALS ON AN ENERGETIC LEVEL

Crystals and precious stones have been valued throughout world cultures over many centuries for their healing virtues, as well as their capacities to imbue strength, courage, clairvoyance, love, tranquillity, and numerous other qualities. Gemstones can help us attune to higher vibrations and bring them into our own experience and being. This theory of crystal resonance suggests that the characteristic energy patterns emanated by any stone can be transferred into the 'liquid crystal medium' of our bodies through resonance. Our bodies, being composed of these tuneable liquids, can mimic and mirror any consistent vibrational pattern with which we come into contact; we can therefore resonate with the healthful qualities of various crystals and minerals. Wearing gemstones is one of the simplest and most effective self-healing practices you can undertake and wearing or carrying those stones whose vibrations correspond with the qualities you wish to embody brings their energetic currents into engagement with your body.

Over time the phenomenon of energetic integration, may be felt tangibly and your own vibrational field may internalise the stone's currents and effectively 'store' them and adjust to them, making them, eventually, a part of your own vibrational make-up. And we seem to know from the resonances we feel within our bodies when in contact with these gemstones, that crystals emanate tangible, if oft immeasurable, currents.

* Manmade and artificially dyed crystals are spiritually 'dead' so use them only for decoration or adornment

CRYSTAL CLEANSING

All crystals have an energy of their own. The animist view of life sees the whole of the natural creation as a living, breathing, intelligent being. All nature's kingdoms, from humans to other animals, plants and minerals, possess varying degrees of intelligence. If you can understand that a human being has a physical body as well as an energy body (or aura), which emanates beyond the physical body, you could extend that idea to our planet Earth. The solid rock of the Earth - the mineral kingdom - forms its physical body, but the Earth also has an energy body which emanates for many kilometres beyond its surface. This 'Earth aura', an electromagnetic field, produces the force we call gravity, which keeps all of us in the plant, animal and human kingdom grounded. Crystals are part of the Earth's structure and are therefore a part of this intelligent force-field. Because we are aware that gemstones are not merely inanimate lumps of rock, but energy in a crystallised form, it is easy to comprehend why the major property of crystals is their ability to receive, store and transmit energy. It is precisely this property which necessitates keeping your crystals clear and cleansed. In short, crystals absorb and transfer energy.

Most crystals, particularly if they are not kept for ornamental purposes and actually used, need to be regularly cleansed. This purification process is especially important if you are dedicating your crystal to a specific intention. If you are going to charge your crystal with a specific thought form to achieve a specific purpose, you must clear it first of all previous vibrations. When you imprint a strong thought form into a virgin clear crystal, the stone can emit a clear one-pointed signal which works quickly and effectively to achieve your goal. Once your goal has been achieved, and you desire to imprint your crystal with a new purpose, you must first de-charge it, and cleanse and purify it using your preferred method, before attempting to re-program it.

Additionally, when many gems are first mined, they are often encrusted with various forms of mineral matter which is removed by placing the crystals in a special solution. But from that point onward, the crystals are handled by numerous individuals, each leaving their own mental or emotional imprint on them. For this reason, stones should always be cleansed after you have purchased or acquired them. Cleansing is also useful for purifying the stone of any energies it may have picked up while being worked with. For example, some crystals are very absorbent, and soak up energies like a sponge, so may need to be cleansed after each use, not just at the time of the Full Moon or whenever convenient for you. You can research the cleansing needs of individual stones in more depth to suit yourself and the unique needs of each stone (e.g. some are more 'absorbent' than others).

Before cleansing any crystal, ensure that the sensitivity of the crystal will not be adversely affected by too much light and/or heat, or immersion in water.

Crystals can be cleansed by any of the following methods:

THE SUN ★ The most powerful natural source of light and energy available to us is Solar radiation, which contains the full spectrum of visible and invisible (ultraviolet and infrared) light. Remember that crystals are literally frozen fire, therefore they love sunlight. For this method, all you need to do is run your crystal under running water, then simply place it outside in the sunlight to air-dry. About half an hour is ideal, as you don't want to damage your crystal in any way. By exposing your crystals to sunlight, you will find that they absorb and store that powerful Solar energy, and when you bring them inside, they will radiate that energy into your room.

THE MOON ★ The Moon's more subtle and ethereal Sun-reflected light can recharge and cleanse crystals. This is a popular, well-known and effective stone-cleansing technique.

SMUDGING / INCENSE ★ Smudging involves burning incense or specially prepared smudge sticks and passing your gemstones through their smoke or using a feather to fan the smoke across the crystals for around 30 seconds. This purifies and clears the stored energies in the crystals, as well as the air around them. Recommended sticks for this purpose are sage, sandalwood, cedarwood or sweetgrass.

ROCK SALT ★ Rock salt is another popular and well-known cleansing technique. Place your crystals on a bed of rock or sea salt and leave overnight under a Full Moon. Leave the salt dry; do not add water.

CRYSTAL TUNING FORK ★ An unusual and little known method of clearing crystals is using a crystal tuning fork, which, as the name suggests, is designed specifically for this purpose. These are high-pitched tuning forks, tuned to around 4096 decibels, especially made to break up energy blockages in gems and crystals. (They can also facilitate the release of the crystals' properties into the atmosphere, which is great for gem therapists, diviners and healers.)

THE FIRE ELEMENT ★ Fire is not used very often in crystal-cleansing but can be very powerful and effective. Find a special place to build a fire (or if that is not possible, light a candle) with the specific intention of purifying your gemstone. Light your fire and mentally call upon the assistance of the spirit of Fire (the Salamanders or likewise) and then pass your crystal through the flames. You will usually find that after doing this a layer of black soot may have formed on the surface of your crystal; this should be easily removed by running it under water, which adds to the power as now you have a doubly purified crystal.

THE EARTH ELEMENT ★ The telluric energy of the Earth has a regenerative and restorative effect on crystals. All you need to do is dig a hole in some clean, unaffected soil (use your instincts to guide you) and bury the crystal or crystals, cover them over with the dirt and then leave overnight, or longer if you wish. One effective method is to bury the crystal at the root of a special tree *, and to ask the tree (along with the Earth) to help purify the crystal. When you dig it up again, the gemstone should be sparkling clear and vibrant. If you can find a remote place where nature is untouched to bury your crystal then the purification will be even more powerful.

THE AIR ELEMENT ★ This method of purification is favoured by the Native American Indians and is otherwise known as 'smudging'. Cleansing with the Air element requires a little more preparation than the others, as you will need to obtain some charcoal blocks and some herbs and incenses to burn on the charcoal. If possible, obtain some frankincense, as this is by far the best all-round incense for purification. Otherwise, cedar, sage and rosemary all work well for purification purposes too. Get your piece of charcoal glowing, sprinkle a little incense upon it, and hold your crystal in the smoke and fumes from the incense as it rises, thereby effectively cleansing and purifying your gemstone.

THE WATER ELEMENT ★ Always use cold water, never hot, and it should be fresh, natural and uncontaminated with no chemical additives. Fresh spring water, seawater or rock salt dissolved in water are all ideal. You can obtain a bottle of sea water and pour it into a bowl containing your crystal. Leave the crystal in the water overnight and in the morning remove your purified crystal and pour the dirty water which has absorbed the negativity into running water and know that it will find its way back to the sea to be dissolved and purified. The ocean is the purification mechanism for this planet; after all, salt water covers two thirds of the land mass, and is a natural absorber and dissolver of energy. Alternatively, you can hold your crystals under running water for a couple of minutes.

ANOTHER CRYSTAL★ Clusters are an excellent method for cleansing your crystals. Quartz clusters in particular, such as those of citrine, clear, smoky or amethyst, are effective at recharging your gemstones. Simply place the crystal on a piece of amethyst or other quartz for around 24 - 48 hours (even less if using clear quartz as the cleanser) to clean and recharge it, as well as to augment the various properties of the gemstone. The crystal bed or geode that you place your crystal/s upon will absorb any negative energy from the crystals, neutralise it, and then reprogram the gems with positive energy.

* UNDER A SPECIAL TREE ★ (Also related to the Earth element) To imbue, energise or re-charge your crystal or crystals with a special, sacred power, you could try burying it in the soil near the roots of a tree that is significant to you. Perhaps you could try your zodiac sign's special tree:

ARIES ✷ Mahogany
TAURUS ✷ Sycamore

GEMINI ✶ Elder
CANCER ✶ Birch
LEO ✶ Walnut
VIRGO ✶ Elder
LIBRA ✶ Sycamore
SCORPIO ✶ Mahogany
SAGITTARIUS ✶ Oak
CAPRICORN ✶ Ebony
AQUARIUS ✶ Pine
PISCES ✶ Oak

There may be other cleansing methods you can think of. I believe that the only limit is your imagination!

CRYSTALS THAT DETERIORATE IN WATER

Do not put the following crystals in water *: Calcite, Carnelian, Hematite, Labradorite, Celestite, Marcasite, Orthoclase, Opal, Lapis Lazuli, Malachite, Selenite (Gypsum), Turquoise, and most clusters.

When cleansing your crystals under the Lunar rays of a Full Moon, it is recommended by many sources to immerse your crystals in spring or seawater, but for some, this can spell the end, or at the very least dull their lustre. So always check first. I learned this the hard way when I tried this method with a beautiful, glossy, tumbled piece of malachite - the water I placed it in irretrievably stole its sheen.

If you do happen to ruin a crystal by using an unsuitable cleansing or re-charging method, my best advice is to bid it farewell, thank it for its service to you, and then bury it in the Earth or throw it in a river or ocean, so that it may return to Source and regenerate itself into a new cycle of life.

* This list is not extensive, and certainly doesn't include every gemstone which should not be cleansed using water. If it is a special crystal and you don't wish to risk ruining it, do your research beforehand! Or, err on the side of caution and use another, safer method such as Full Moon cleansing.

CHAPTER TWO
★
CLEAR QUARTZ ~ THE MASTER CRYSTAL

★ CLEAR QUARTZ ★

Power Crystal for all Zodiac Signs, Chakras, Ailments & Conditions

♈ ♉ ♊ ♋ ♌ ♍ ♎ ♏ ♐ ♑ ♒ ♓

★ QUARTZ ~ CLEAR QUARTZ ★

Class ★ Silicate
Crystalline Form ★ Hexagonal
Mohs Scale Hardness ★ 7
Colour ★ Colourless
Chakra ★ Crown
Clarity & Brilliance ★ From clear to opaque

Main Spiritual & Metaphysical Qualities ★ Good for meditation; brings balance to thoughts & feelings; aids the opening of the mind to higher levels of reality; cleansing; harmonising; purifying; master healer on all levels.

Astrological Affinities ★ Sun, Jupiter, All Zodiac Signs

Magical Tips ★ Single quartz crystals are used for directing a stream of energy between all the chakras. Simply point the end of the crystal in the direction in which you wish the energy force to flow. Clear Quartz amplifies the magic of any work you do or wishes you make and is thought to be the only crystal that is modifiable or 'programmable' to suit your own personal needs and desires. Simply program your special crystal with your specific intention or purpose, using the information box following 'Programming Your Unique Quartz Crystal'.

Vibration ★ Earthy & High

Otherwise known as rock crystal, this is truly the supreme healer of the crystal world, the perfect all-rounder with wide-ranging healing applications. The word crystal comes from the Greek word *krystallos*, meaning ice, and clear quartz indeed resembles ice closely.

When people think about crystals, pure quartz is usually the first one to come to mind. Quartz is known as 'the salt of the earth', and for good reason. It is composed of silica ~ the most common and abundant mineral compound on our planet.

The six sides of a quartz crystal represent the first six chakras. The sides come together in a point, symbolising the seventh or Crown chakra. This is our connection with the Infinite Divine. Quartz crystals, in their perfect form, look like pyramids, which are also instruments that enable high frequency energies to manifest themselves in physical reality.

Quartz, named after a Slavic word for 'hard', is the crystalline form of silicon, and many popular gems, such as clear crystal, amethyst, tiger's eye, citrine, aventurine and carnelian, are from the quartz family. Each type of quartz has different properties and characteristics, but as a gem family, they all bring transition, change, and high frequencies that can effect deep health, healing, and overall wellbeing.

Of all the quartz family, the clear variety is known as the Master Healer. Because it is free of colour vibrations, it is open to suggestion, which is known as programming, and you can program a quartz with your consciousness to perform any activity or function you wish.

A common, well-known and popular gem, clear quartz is an all-purpose 'jack-of-all-trades' stone. It is a frequency-increasing stone for each of the chakra centres and will allow you to access high levels of information both spiritually and on the physical plane. As it is connected with all the energy bodies, it increases the power of all other stones.

Clear quartz is also a deep soul cleanser, which unblocks and regulates energy and emotions on every level. It reflects clear white light that can be directed to everyday thoughts, feelings, words and situations. Clear quartz has a tremendous ability to vibrate on the levels of colour frequencies, which demonstrates how clarity and purity can enter into even the darker and lower frequencies. These crystals prove that all the chakras can indeed vibrate at once and still work together with light. Quartz can bring the aura to a very high frequency and, in this process, all colours of the aura get brighter.

Although clear quartz is often described as frozen water, it would be much more appropriate to describe it as frozen fire. The source of all light, fire and energy on our planet is the Sun, the centre of our Solar system. Through their formation under intense heat in beds of igneous volcanic rock, clear quartz crystals seem to embody this fiery principle.

The astrological rulership (the ruling planets assigned to everything in nature, according to its rate of vibration or Mohs scale of hardness) given to clear quartz is, as well as being aligned with all zodiac signs and planetary bodies, more specifically the Sun and Jupiter, both fiery planets. It is this ability of rock crystal to receive, store and transmit the Solar life-force that makes it such a versatile and beneficial tool in healing.

Clear quartz is thought to be the only crystal that is modifiable or 'programmable' to suit your needs, as other crystals automatically contain their own specific resonance or natural signature. In ancient times quartz was thought of as a permanent form of ice, its clarity and purity having magical similarities to water and glass. Because it contains the full spectrum of the visible white light, it is truly an all-purpose healing tool, containing a broad spectrum energy which clears dis-ease and disharmony on all levels. Clear quartz stabilises, focuses and amplifies the vital life-force, and its resonance will swiftly go to any area/s in need of healing or restructuring. It also activates, amplifies and channels the magic of any work you do or wishes you make, by receiving, storing, transforming, transmitting and magnifying all energy and thought forms.

Kirlian photography ** has revealed that when a quartz crystal is held in the hand, the strength of the biomagnetic energy field is at least doubled. It therefore follows that placing one on any part of the body will increase the energy in that area. Its vibrations, which begin at about room temperature, give this mineral an important role in all holistic practice, and whether held in the hand, placed on a person, or positioned in close proximity to any living thing, clear quartz enlarges the aura of everything near it, even increasing the healing powers of other minerals. Many healers find they obtain swifter results when the patient holds a piece of clear quartz.

It was, and still is, the stone most favoured for crystal gazing or scrying, for its lustre quickly 'freezes' the optic nerve, with the result that outside, 'external' impressions are suspended and the eye is 'released' to gaze into its depths. It is balancing and harmonising and can attune you to your spiritual purpose. Rock crystal is believed to strengthen the link between Earth and the heavens, enabling its user to see into other times and places, so it is a useful aid for psychic travelling and dream journeys.

Contrary to generally held belief, quartz crystals are not energised by the Sun, although they can be utilised to concentrate its rays. It is the Moon which stimulates the energy field of a quartz crystal, for as it is drawn even closer by the gravitational pull of the Earth, as happens at the time of the Full Moon, its close proximity stimulates all magnetic fields. Indeed, clear quartz, the Master Healer of the crystal Universe, is a mineral which is closely allied to the energies of the Moon, whose effect upon sensitive individuals is well-known. (Likewise, the energy flow of clear quartz, and many other crystals, will appear to ebb and flow in accordance with the phases of the Moon, reaching a peak when the Moon is full.)

Rock quartz crystals are geometric structures that are naturally aligned with the Earth's magnetic fields. The energy they attract to themselves from such fields, combined with their own inbuilt electromagnetic force, provides a powerful form of stimulus, which is wonderfully beneficial to anyone who is physically depleted. When this vitalising force is consciously introduced into the etheric body, or electromagnetic field of any individual, it results in an almost instantaneous restoration of bodily energy. Clear quartz therefore provides a powerful healing force, one which all therapists involved in the healing arts are recommended to utilise. Clear quartz has long been known to produce a natural harmony between people and the electromagnetic energies which continually flow through the ethers. These in turn aid the formation of the positive and negative ions, which are so essential to enhanced and continuous collective and personal wellbeing.

In various cultures, quartz crystal is reputed to be the most powerful crystal, the 'grandfather crystal', and the 'chief of the Stone People'. Because of its all-encompassing nature and wide-ranging healing abilities, it has zodiacal affinities with all the signs and planetary bodies.

** Kirlian photography is a technique of photography that captures the electrical field that radiates from organic matter and the bio magnetic sheath or aura surrounding the body.

PROGRAMMING YOUR UNIQUE QUARTZ CRYSTAL

Quartz crystal has an aura. Just as every living, intelligent life-form in the natural Universe partakes of the life force and emanates its own electromagnetic field, or aura, crystals are no exception. Clear quartz crystals are attuned to the core magnetic energy of the Earth and owing to its affinity with the Fire principle in nature, it is a very efficient conductor of the Solar life force, which is why it resonates with all zodiac signs and planetary bodies. Clear quartz is thought to be the only crystal that is modifiable or 'programmable' to suit your needs *, as other crystals automatically contain their own specific resonance or natural signature. In essence, clear quartz is the most easily programmable and the most overall healing of crystals and holds a unique importance in the Universe of gems. From all forms of natural rock quartz flows a continual stream of electromagnetic energy, which is released into the atmosphere to benefit all life forms.

* To program your clear quartz crystal, simply hold it on your Third Eye chakra (between and just above the physical eyes) and concentrate on the purpose for which you wish to use it. Be positive and receptive while you allow your crystal to fill with this energy. If you wish, you could also state the intention of the programming out loud, for example, 'I program this crystal for love', healing, meditation, abundance, protection or (insert your own word here)'. You could also run your clear quartz crystal under running water, allow it to dry naturally, then hold the stone with both hands, bring it up to your mouth and blow into it sharply three times in order to impregnate it with your own breath. Then, hold it firmly in one hand and silently invite and welcome it into your life as a friend, helper and guide.

CHAPTER THREE
★
CRYSTALS & ASTROLOGY

The ancients held that every gem was originally crystallised by and around an entity ... capable of impressing the subconscious mind of the person possessing the gem as to coming events, thereby enabling him to avoid danger and to enhance opportunities. Hence, the importance of wearing jewels in harmony with one's stellar rays.

Corinne Heline

GEMSTONES FOR THE BIRTH MONTHS

January ★ Garnet, Rose Quartz, Zircon, Turquoise, Amber
February ★ Amethyst, Hyacinth, Onyx, Pearl, Moonstone, Bloodstone
March ★ Aquamarine, Bloodstone, Jasper, Jade
April ★ Diamond, Clear Quartz, Sapphire, Zircon
May ★ Emerald, Chrysoprase, Agate, Tourmaline
June ★ Pearl, Moonstone, Emerald, Agate
July ★ Ruby, Onyx, Turquoise, Carnelian
August ★ Peridot, Sardonyx, Carnelian, Moonstone
September ★ Sapphire, Lapis Lazuli, Peridot
October ★ Opal, Tourmaline, Aquamarine
November ★ Topaz, Citrine
December ★ Tanzanite, Ruby, Turquoise, Chrysoprase

CRYSTALS & THE PLANETS

All the Vedic texts agree in relating gems to planets. This verse from the *Jatax Parijat* links each gem to a planet:

'The ruby is the gem of the Lord of the Day (the Sun),
The shining pearly is the gem of the cold Moon,
Red coral is the gem of Mars,
The emerald is the gem of noble Mercury,
Yellow sapphire is the gem of Jupiter, instructor of gods,
Diamond is the gem of Venus, instructor of demons,
Blue sapphire is the gem of Saturn.'

Each planet influence its gem, and their curative power varies according to the position of its planet in the zodiac. Ayurvedic medicine has always paid attention to these details in their healing practices, often advising people to wear their corresponding zodiacal stone as a ring or a talisman.

THE CRYSTALLINE SYSTEM OF THE SUN

Associated with the Sun are Amber, Chrysolite, Diamond, Onyx, Ruby, Topaz and Fluorite. The Sun is represented by the crystalline system known as cubic, which is a cubic shape as the name suggests. The stone most representative of this system is Fluorite, which in ancient times was reputed to strengthen thinking, the powers of concentration and reflection, and to bring peace and calm to the minds of those who wore it.

THE SUN'S GEMSTONE ASSOCIATION ★ Ruby

THE CRYSTALLINE SYSTEM OF THE MOON

Associated with the Moon are Aquamarine, Opal, Clear Quartz, Emerald, Diamond, Selenite and of course, Moonstone. The Moon is represented by the fourth crystalline system, known as hexagonal. The stone which perhaps represents this system best, the Emerald, or aluminium and beryllium silicate, was always regarded as having sacred qualities in ancient times. Its uses in ophthalmology, to prevent bleeding, for liver complaints, and as an antiseptic, were well-known, as was its power to stimulate the memory, which is analogous with the Moon.

THE MOON'S GEMSTONE ASSOCIATION ★ Pearl

THE CRYSTALLINE SYSTEM OF MERCURY

Associated with Mercury are Tiger's Eye, Jasper, Agate, Coral, Beryl, Azurite, Sardonyx, Gypsum and Marcasite. This is the seventh crystalline system, which is analogous with Mercury, and is known as the monoclinical or clinorhombic system, that is having an oblique prism on a diamond-shaped base. The stone which perhaps represents this system best is Azurite, or copper hydrocarbonate.

MERCURY'S GEMSTONE ASSOCIATION ★ Emerald

THE CRYSTALLINE SYSTEM OF VENUS

Associated with Venus are Emerald, Pink Coral, Lapis Lazuli, Agate, Beryl, Amazonite, Albite, Pearl, Aquamarine and Light Sapphire. Venus is represented by the sixth crystalline system, known as triclinical, that is having a parallelepiped on a diamond-shaped base. The stone which perhaps represents this system best, the Amazonite, or aluminium and potassium double silicate, is a brilliant example of it. Analogous with Venus, the triclinical Amazonite had qualities of bringing hope and love to those who wore it.

VENUS'S GEMSTONE ASSOCIATION ★ Diamond

THE CRYSTALLINE SYSTEM OF MARS

Associated with Mars are Amethyst, Magnetite, Cornelian, Barite, Garnet, Ruby, Topaz and Bloodstone. Mars is represented by the third crystalline system, known as orthorhombic, that is having a rectangular parallelepiped. The stone which perhaps represents this system best is Topaz, which was famous for the good fortune it brought to those who wore it, but also for its therapeutic properties in treating and even healing eye-related conditions.

MARS'S GEMSTONE ASSOCIATION ★ Red Coral

THE CRYSTALLINE SYSTEM OF JUPITER

Yonder, is the Mountain of Amethyst. It links with the higher octaves of Sagittarius and is a sign of wisdom gained. The stone has many virtues. It bestows tranquillity and induces mental clarity and prevision. What is more, it protects the traveller and is a bringer of light at any level. The beings you see within it are the elementals of the Earth Plane, who are under the protection of their benefactor, great Jupiter.

Patricia Crowther

Associated with Jupiter are Amethyst, Beryl, Emerald, Sapphire and Turquoise. Jupiter is represented by the fifth crystalline system, known as the rhomboidric system, that is having a parallelepiped whose six sides are diamond-shaped and of equal size, ideally represented by the Rhodochrosite or magnesium carbonate. This, it has been suggested, has a curative action on such Jupiterian afflictions as liver complaints, ulcers, asthma and congestion.

JUPITER'S GEMSTONE ASSOCIATION ★ Yellow Sapphire

THE CRYSTALLINE SYSTEM OF SATURN

Associated with Saturn are Black Coral, Carnelian, Jet, Onyx and Black Pearl. Saturn is represented by the second crystalline system, known as quadratic, that is having an upright prism with a square base, and its characteristics seem to be connected with this planet. The stone which perhaps represents this system best, the Wulfenite (only relatively recently discovered), is nothing other than lead molybdate, which is analogous with Saturn.

SATURN'S GEMSTONE ASSOCIATION ★ Blue Sapphire

CRYSTALS & THE MONTHS

Each month's traditional birthstone, and the meaning * the ancients ascribed to it:

January ★ Garnet, emblem of constancy, sincerity, friendliness, frankness, generosity.
February ★ Amethyst, emblem of sincerity. Helps with alcoholism, creates contentment, draws favour from superiors.
March ★ Bloodstone, emblem of courage.
April ★ Diamond, emblem of innocence. Reconciles lovers, gives constancy, fidelity, innocence. Diamonds are unconquerable and impart courage and faith.
May ★ Emerald, emblem of love success. Strengthens love and intelligence, eloquence, popularity.
June ★ Agate, emblem of health and longevity.
July ★ Carnelian, emblem of contentment.
August ★ Sardonyx, emblem of marital happiness. Gives intellectual power, can be used in magical rites.
September ★ Chrysolite, emblem of protection from insanity.
October ★ Opal, emblem of hope.
November ★ Topaz, emblem of fidelity. Gives sobriety, fidelity, love, draws honour or wealth, cures anger.
December ★ Turquoise, emblem of prosperity. Prevents accidents, brings safety.

* From the *Complete Book of Magic and Witchcraft*, 1986, Leonard R.N. Ashley

CRYSTALS & THE SEASONS

The Magic of 'Precious Stones'

The term 'precious stone' is generally used to denote diamond, emerald, sapphire, ruby and, more recently, pearl. It is interesting to note that all the crystals classified as 'precious' are also the hardest on the Mohs scale. Pearl is not as hard as the others (which all score between 8 and 10), but earns the title due to its desirability, popularity, and beauty. Since ancient times, the traditional four precious stones have also been associated with the seasons. Sometimes called 'ice' because of its icy, cold beauty, diamonds represent winter; the deep green of emerald represents spring; the brilliant red of ruby represents summer; and the pure blue of sapphire represents the rains of autumn.

GEMSTONES OF THE ZODIAC

Aries ★ Bloodstone, Carnelian, Diamond, Aquamarine, Aventurine, Hematite, Lapis Lazuli, Malachite, Obsidian
Taurus ★ Rose Quartz, Diamond, Sapphire, Emerald, Jade, Selenite, Carnelian
Gemini ★ Citrine, Tiger's Eye, Agate, Alexandrite, Aquamarine, Jade
Cancer ★ Emerald, Chrysoprase, Moonstone, Pearl, Ruby, Aventurine, Carnelian
Leo ★ Clear Quartz, Onyx, Citrine, Ruby, Peridot, Carnelian, Jasper, White Onyx
Virgo ★ Carnelian, Sapphire, Peridot, Sardonyx, Agate
Libra ★ Peridot, Jacinth, Tourmaline, Opal, Sapphire, Aventurine, Chrysoprase, Citrine, Jade, Moonstone, Rose Quartz
Scorpio ★ Aquamarine, Topaz, Malachite, Peridot, Labradorite, Moonstone, Turquoise
Sagittarius ★ Topaz, Zircon, Turquoise, Amethyst, Azurite, Labradorite, Obsidian, Smoky Quartz
Capricorn ★ Ruby, Garnet, Turquoise, Smoky Quartz, Fluorite, Amethyst, Tiger's Eye
Aquarius ★ Garnet, Turquoise, Aquamarine, Amethyst, Azurite, Hematite, Lapis Lazuli
Pisces ★ Amethyst, Bloodstone, Turquoise, Aquamarine, Blue Lace Agate, Chrysoprase, Fluorite

MYSTICAL BIRTHSTONES OF THE ZODIAC

Aries ✯ Jade
Taurus ✯ Opal
Gemini ✯ Sapphire
Cancer ✯ Moonstone
Leo ✯ Ruby
Virgo ✯ Diamond
Libra ✯ Agate
Scorpio ✯ Jasper
Sagittarius ✯ Pearl
Capricorn ✯ Onyx
Aquarius ✯ Emerald
Pisces ✯ Bloodstone

ARIEN & MARTIAN LUCKY CRYSTALS, STONES & GEMS

ARIES BIRTH STONES ★ Ruby, Bloodstone, Aquamarine, Diamond
MARCH BIRTH STONES ★ Jasper, Bloodstone, Aquamarine
APRIL BIRTH STONES ★ Sapphire, Diamond, Zircon

Ruby, Bloodstone, Aquamarine and Diamond (Aries's four primary birthstones), Red Coral (for Mars), Jasper, Sapphire and Zircon (March and April birthstones) are your luckiest stones, and one of these gems should be worn about your person to ensure good luck and increase your magnetism. Hematite, Iron Pyrite, Magnetite, Aventurine, Carnelian, Fire Agate, Citrine, Amethyst, Kunzite, Apache Tear, Kyanite, Flint, Tibetan Quartz, Malachite, Rhodochrosite, Mahogany Obsidian, Lapis Lazuli, Titanium Quartz, Emerald, Tektite, Orange Spinel, Topaz, Garnet, Red Jasper and Pink Tourmaline also align with Aries' energy.

TAUREAN & VENUSIAN LUCKY CRYSTALS, STONES & GEMS

TAURUS BIRTH STONES ★ Diamond, Sapphire, Emerald
APRIL BIRTH STONES ★ Sapphire, Diamond, Zircon
MAY BIRTH STONES ★ Agate, Emerald, Tourmaline, Chrysoprase

Diamond, Sapphire, Emerald (Taurus's four primary birthstones), Jade, Rose Quartz (Venusian gems), Zircon, Agate, Tourmaline and

Chrysoprase (April and May birthstones) are your luckiest stones, and one or more of these gems should be worn about your person to ensure good luck and increase your magnetism. Lapis Lazuli, Coral, Moss Agate, Aquamarine, Boji Stone, Copper, Topaz, Carnelian, Azurite, Chrysocolla, Variscite, Malachite, Kyanite, Tibetan Quartz, Amazonite, Green Aventurine, Green Calcite, Olivine, Spinel, Titanium Quartz, Selenite, Rhodonite and Tiger's Eye also align with Taurean energy.

GEMINIAN & MERCURIAL LUCKY CRYSTALS, STONES & GEMS

GEMINI BIRTH STONES ★ Alexandrite, Agate, Citrine
MAY BIRTH STONES ★ Agate, Emerald, Tourmaline, Chrysoprase
JUNE BIRTH STONES ★ Emerald, Pearl, Moonstone

Alexandrite, Agate, Citrine (Gemini's three primary birthstones), Emerald (Mercury), Tourmaline, Chrysoprase, Pearl and Moonstone (May and June birthstones) are your luckiest stones, and at least one of these gems should be worn about your person to ensure good luck and increase your overall magnetism. Serpentine, Hematite, Aquamarine, Calcite, Tiger's Eye, Chrysocolla, Apophyllite, Noble or Iridescent Opal, Rainbow Quartz, Hyaline Quartz, Apatite, Celestine, Celestite, Marble, Tibetan Quartz, Titanium Quartz, Blue Spinel, Goldstone, Green Obsidian, Zoisite, Variscite, Topaz, Ulexite, Epidote, Dendritic Agate, Sapphire, Tourmilated and Rutilated Quartz, Jade, Diamond, and all gems that sparkle brilliantly are also in harmony with Geminian energy.

CANCERIAN & LUNAR LUCKY CRYSTALS, STONES & GEMS

CANCER BIRTH STONES ★ Moonstone, Pearl, Ruby
JUNE BIRTH STONES ★ Emerald, Pearl, Moonstone
JULY BIRTH STONES ★ Onyx, Ruby, Turquoise, Carnelian

Moonstone, Pearl, Ruby (Cancer's three primary birthstones), Emerald, Onyx, Turquoise and Carnelian (June and July birthstones) are your luckiest stones, and at least one of these gems should be worn about your person to ensure good luck and increase your overall magnetism. Fire Agate, Moss Agate, Dendritic Agate, Beryl, Rhodonite, Aventurine,

Opal, Amber, Brown Spinel, Chrysoprase, Pink Tourmaline, Green Garnet Grossularite, Blue Agate, White Onyx, Snowflake Obsidian, Tibetan Quartz, Titanium Quartz, Tektite, and Calcite (green, blue and orange), also align with Cancerian energy.

LEONINE & SOLAR LUCKY CRYSTALS, STONES & GEMS

LEO BIRTH STONES ★ Citrine, Ruby, Peridot
JULY BIRTH STONES ★ Onyx, Turquoise, Ruby, Carnelian
AUGUST BIRTH STONES ★ Carnelian, Moonstone, Peridot, Sardonyx

Citrine, Ruby, Peridot (Leo's three primary birthstones), Onyx, Turquoise, Carnelian, Moonstone and Sardonyx (July and August birth stones) are your luckiest stones, and one or more of these gems should be worn about your person to ensure good luck and increase your magnetism. Boji Stone, Fire Agate, Diamond, Amber, Chrysolite, Cat's Eye, Golden Beryl *, Yellow Spinel, Garnet, Chrysocolla, Tiger's Eye, Kunzite, Sunstone, Emerald, Green and Pink Tourmaline, Orange Calcite, Yellow Calcite, Larimar ^, Petalite, Clear Quartz, Tibetan Quartz, Pyrite, Labradorite, Titanium Quartz, Yellow Sapphire, Aqua Aura, Red Obsidian, Golden Topaz, Heliodor, Rhodochrosite, and all yellow/orange stones also align with Leonine energy. To bring about even greater luck these stones should be set in gold, since this is the metal of the Sun, ruler of Leo.

^ Larimar is a beautiful blue, white, and sometimes green stone found in only one mine in the world. Discovered in the early 1970s, the name Larimar comes from "Larissa", the name of the miner's daughter, and "mar", meaning sea. A rare and powerfully healing gem, it is prized by psychics and healers throughout the world.

* Golden Beryl is often called 'the sunshine stone', because it is the ultimate confidence, possibility and wellbeing gem.

VIRGOAN & MERCURIAL LUCKY CRYSTALS, STONES & GEMS

VIRGO BIRTH STONES ★ Sapphire, Carnelian, Peridot, Sardonyx
AUGUST BIRTH STONES ★ Peridot, Sardonyx, Moonstone, Carnelian
SEPTEMBER BIRTH STONES ★ Peridot, Sapphire, Lapis Lazuli

Sapphire, Carnelian, Peridot, Sardonyx (Virgo's four primary birthstones), Moonstone, Lapis Lazuli (August and September birthstones), and Emerald (Mercury) are your luckiest stones, and one or more of these gems should be worn about your person to ensure good luck and increase your magnetism. Banded Agate, Jade, Diamond, Jasper, Rutilated Quartz, Amazonite, Citrine, Opal, Magnetite, Blue Topaz, Smithsonite, Moss Agate, Rubellite, Purple Obsidian, Sodalite, Sugilite, Dioptase, Chrysocolla, Amethyst, True Jasper, Snowflake Obsidian, Cat's Eye, Hawk's Eye, Grey Onyx, Grey Amber, Alexandrite and Garnet also align with Virgo's energy.

LIBRAN & VENUSIAN LUCKY CRYSTALS, STONES & GEMS

LIBRA BIRTH STONES ★ Opal, Tourmaline, Sapphire
SEPTEMBER BIRTH STONES ★ Peridot, Sapphire, Lapis Lazuli
OCTOBER BIRTH STONES ★ Opal, Aquamarine, Tourmaline

Opal, Tourmaline, Sapphire (Libra's three primary birthstones), Jade, Rose Quartz, Diamond (Venusian gems), Peridot, Sapphire, Aquamarine and Lapis Lazuli (September and October birthstones) are your luckiest stones, and one or more of these gems should be worn about your person to ensure good luck and increase your magnetism. Moonstone, Green Tourmaline, Marble, Sardonyx, Jacinth, Sunstone, Topaz, Kunzite, Mahogany Obsidian, Ametrine, Aventurine, Chrysoprase, Citrine, Moss Agate, Amazonite, Malachite, Nephrite (Jade), Bloodstone, Kyanite, Apophyllite, Tibetan Quartz, Titanium Quartz and Green Spinel also align with Libra's energy.

SCORPION & PLUTONIAN LUCKY CRYSTALS, STONES & GEMS

SCORPIO BIRTH STONES ★ Topaz, Malachite, Peridot
OCTOBER BIRTH STONES ★ Opal, Aquamarine, Tourmaline
NOVEMBER BIRTH STONES ★ Topaz, Citrine, Pearl

Topaz, Malachite, Peridot (Scorpio's three primary birthstones), Opal, Aquamarine, Tourmaline, Citrine, Pearl (October and November birthstones), and Red Coral (Mars) are your luckiest stones, and one or more of these gems should be worn about your person to ensure good luck and increase your overall magnetism. Labradorite, Hematite, Carnelian, Moonstone, Turquoise, Magnetite, Ruby, Beryl, Red Spinel,

Rhodochrosite, Emerald, Apache Tear, Obsidian, Hiddenite, Stibnite, Tibetan Quartz, Titanium Quartz, Variscite, Boji Stone, Flint, Shiva Lingam, Dioptase, Green Tourmaline, True Jasper, Yellow Calcite, Iron Tiger's Eye, Red Jasper, Jacinth, Black Tourmaline, Sunstone, Red Amber, Garnet, Kunzite and Herkimer Diamond also align with Scorpio's energy. Additionally, all scarlet and dark red stones are especially beneficial attractors for Scorpios.

SAGITTARIAN & JUPITERIAN LUCKY CRYSTALS, STONES & GEMS

SAGITTARIUS BIRTH STONES ★ Topaz, Turquoise, Zircon
NOVEMBER BIRTH STONES ★ Topaz, Citrine, Pearl
DECEMBER BIRTH STONES ★ Ruby, Turquoise, Bloodstone, Lapis Lazuli, Zircon, Tanzanite (modern)

Topaz, Turquoise, Zircon (Sagittarius's three primary birthstones), Yellow Sapphire, Amethyst (Jupiter), Ruby, Bloodstone, Citrine, Pearl, Lapis Lazuli and Tanzanite (November and December birthstones) are your luckiest stones, and one or more of these gems should be worn about your person to ensure good luck and increase your magnetism. Dark Blue Spinel, Azurite, Labradorite, Smoky Quartz, Lazurite, Blue Lace Agate, Dioptase, Gold Obsidian, Cyanite, Garnet, Okenite, Sodalite, Rhodochrosite, Charoite, Snowflake Obsidian, Malachite, Pink Tourmaline and Sugilite also align with Sagittarian energy.

CAPRICORNIAN & SATURNIAN LUCKY CRYSTALS, STONES & GEMS

CAPRICORN BIRTH STONES ★ Garnet, Turquoise, Smoky Quartz, Jet
DECEMBER BIRTH STONES ★ Ruby, Turquoise, Bloodstone, Lapis Lazuli, Zircon, Tanzanite
JANUARY BIRTH STONES ★ Garnet, Zircon

Garnet, Turquoise, Smoky Quartz, Jet (Capricorn's four primary birthstones), Zircon, Ruby (December and January birthstones), and Blue Sapphire (Saturn) are your luckiest stones, and at least one of these gems should be worn about your person to ensure good luck and increase your overall magnetism. Black Coral, White Onyx, Banded Agate, Snowflake Obsidian, Mahogany Obsidian, Black Pearl, Amethyst, Tiger's Eye, Black Onyx, Carnelian, Green and Black

Tourmaline, Hematite, Tibetan Quartz, Titanium Quartz, Aragonite, Malachite, Stibnite, Chalcopyrite, Azurite, Amber, Fluorite, Galena, Labradorite, Magnetite, Clear Quartz and Peridot also align with Capricorn's energy.

AQUARIAN & URANIAN LUCKY CRYSTALS, STONES & GEMS

AQUARIUS BIRTH STONES ★ Amethyst, Garnet, Aquamarine
JANUARY BIRTH STONES ★ Zircon, Garnet
FEBRUARY BIRTH STONES ★ Amethyst, Hyacinth

Amethyst, Garnet, Aquamarine (Aquarius's three primary birthstones), Zircon (January birth stone), Hyacinth (February birth stone), Jacinth, Jargoon (Uranus), and Blue Sapphire (Saturn) are your luckiest gems, and one or more of these gems should be worn about your person to ensure good luck and increase your magnetism. Magnetite, Sugilite, Tourmaline, Dermantine, Apatite, Jade, Diamond, Bixbyite, Blue Obsidian, Lapis Lazuli, Chrysoprase, Blue Celestite, Azurite, Spirit Cactus Quartz, Fuchsite, Boji Stone, Black Pearl, Slate, Hematite, Blue Quartz, Cavansite, Amber (Uranus), Angelite, Blue Lace Agate, Labradorite, Clear Quartz, Moonstone, Imperial Topaz, Fluorite, Antacamite, Tibetan Quartz, Titanium Quartz, Larimar ^ and Turquoise also align with Aquarius's energy.

^ Larimar is a beautiful blue, white, and sometimes green stone found in only one mine in the world. Discovered in the early 1970s, the name Larimar comes from "Larissa", the name of the miner's daughter, and "mar", meaning sea. A rare and powerfully healing gem, it is prized by psychics and healers throughout the world.

PISCEAN & NEPTUNIAN LUCKY CRYSTALS, STONES & GEMS

PISCES BIRTH STONES ★ Amethyst, Turquoise, Aquamarine
FEBRUARY BIRTH STONES ★ Amethyst, Hyacinth
MARCH BIRTH STONES ★ Jasper, Bloodstone, Aquamarine

Amethyst, Turquoise, Aquamarine (Pisces's three primary birthstones), Jasper, Hyacinth, Bloodstone (February and March birthstones), and Yellow Sapphire (Jupiter) are your luckiest stones, and one or more of these gems should be worn about your person to ensure good luck and increase your overall magnetism. Coral, Mother of Pearl and Emerald are also particularly auspicious gemstones for Pisces. Moonstone, Clear Quartz, Labradorite, Fire Agate, Beryl, Staurolite, Chrysoprase, Pumice, Chrysolite, Sugilite, Sand, Blue Lace Agate, Tibetan Quartz, Green Grossular Garnet, Sodalite, Citrine, Titanium Quartz, Chevron Amethyst, Diaspore, Sunstone, Calcite, Tourmaline, Smithsonite, Spessartine, Angelite, Carnelian, Bixbytite, Anglesite, Opal, Smoky Quartz, Green Fluorite, Pearl, Blue Quartz, Milky Quartz, Rose Quartz, Spirit Cactus Quartz, Imperial Topaz, Jade and Larimar ^ also align with Piscean energy.

^ Larimar is a beautiful blue, white, and sometimes green stone found in only one mine in the world. Discovered in the early 1970s, the name Larimar comes from "Larissa", the name of the miner's daughter, and "mar", meaning sea. A rare and powerfully healing gem, it is prized by psychics and healers throughout the world.

CRYSTAL RELATIONSHIPS

The relationships between the planets and gems used in the jewellery, as detailed in the oldest astrological texts, find a logical extension in correspondences with the twelve signs of the zodiac and the principal chakras.

(see next page)

CRYSTAL	COLOUR	PLANET	ZODIAC SIGN	CHAKRA
Amber	Yellow	Sun	Leo	Solar Plexus
Amethyst	Violet	Neptune	Pisces	Third Eye
Aquamarine	Blue	Uranus	Aquarius	Throat
Bloodstone	Green & Red	Venus	Libra	Heart
Carnelian	Red	Pluto	Scorpio	Sacral
Chrysoprase	Red	Pluto	Scorpio	Sacral
Diamond	Colourless	Mercury	Gemini	Crown
Emerald	Green	Venus	Taurus	Heart
Garnet	Red	Mars	Aries	Root
Gold	Yellow	Sun	Leo	Solar Plexus
Hyaline Quartz	Colourless	Mercury	Gemini	Crown
Jade	Green	Venus	Taurus	Heart
Labradorite	Iridescent	Mercury	Virgo	Crown
Lapis Lazuli	Blue	Jupiter	Sagittarius	Third Eye
Malachite	Green	Venus	Libra	Heart
Obsidian	Black	Saturn	Capricorn	Root
Onyx (White)	White	Moon	Cancer	Crown
Onyx (Black)	Black	Saturn	Capricorn	Root
Opal	Iridescent	Mercury	Virgo	Crown
Fire Opal	Red	Pluto	Scorpio	Sacral
Pearl	White	Moon	Cancer	Crown
Red Coral	Red	Mars	Aries	Sacral
Rose Quartz	Pink	Venus	Taurus	Heart
Ruby	Red	Mars	Aries	Sacral
Sapphire	Blue	Jupiter	Sagittarius	Third Eye
Silver	White	Moon	Cancer	Crown
Tiger's Eye	Yellow	Sun	Leo	Solar Plexus
Topaz (Yellow)	Yellow	Sun	Leo	Solar Plexus
Topaz (Blue)	Blue	Uranus	Aquarius	Throat
Tourmaline (Blue)	Blue	Uranus	Aquarius	Throat
Tourmaline (Black)	Black	Saturn	Capricorn	Root
Turquoise	Turquoise	Uranus	Aquarius	Throat

CRYSTALS & THE ELEMENTS

Modern research affirms the ancient teaching that the Universe was created from the four elements of Fire, Air, Water and Earth, in that order, each growing from its predecessor and - if we wish to delve into the mystical realm of metaphysics here - all animated in turn by the Word breathed upon them at the beginning of All That Is. We can interpret Plato's statement, that "gems owe their origins to the stars" as an etheric influence acting on the auriferous matter which forms their composition.

Crystals are inextricably linked to the four elements, from their original creation to their potency and use in magical rituals and healing. Formed by the combination, in varying conditions, of different physical elements, such as metals, non-metals and gases, some stones require the enormous heat generated by volcanoes or deep thermal currents to bond their molecular makeup, while others may require pressure or water sources. The effects of the four elements of Fire, Earth, Air and Water is evident in these formation processes. The heat generated by Fire, pressure from the Earth, and the chemical reactions involved in absorbing elements from the Air and Water, all demonstrate the four elements in action to produce the correct conditions and ingredients necessary for the creation of crystals, lending them each their unique qualities. There is a fifth element: Ether, which is another name for 'spirit', and which is arguably immeasurable, but without which the other four elements cannot effectively function. The effect of Ether in all living things is growth and development. Although this is clearly measurable and visible in animals and plants, it is not so immediately apparent in crystals. Crystals do grow and change with time however and have similar measurable auric fields to animals and plants. Ether is the life force and consciousness that pervades and energises all living things, the invisible essence that bonds the other four together. According to magical beliefs systems, without the energy provided by Ether, matter would simply be inert.

CRYSTALS & THE FIRE ELEMENT

It is almost two million years since humans harnessed one of the great powers of minerals: the ability to produce fire. The ability to create fire with the sparks given off when two very hard stones, such as flint and pyrites, were struck together, was arguably one of the biggest discoveries and 'turning points' in human evolution.

The transformational influence of Fire can be seen in such examples as citrine, which is formed when heat is applied to amethyst, and obsidian, which is created through astonishingly high volcanic temperatures. Although Fire can be a destructive force, its effect is also to change things, and it is this transformative energy that can be harnessed when working with Fire-inspired gemstones to help facilitate positive changes in your life, through meditation, chakra balancing or other magical rituals.

Some Fiery crystals are ★ Calcite, Ruby, Amber, Obsidian, Garnet, Citrine, Bloodstone (Heliotrope), Topaz, Spinel and Pyrite.

CRYSTALS & THE EARTH ELEMENT

The most obvious elemental force for crystals is the Earth, in which they are found. Crystals are formed over millions of years, which naturally links them with Earthy qualities of perseverance, endurance and patience. These gemstones provide the stability of the Earth and the ability to remain, or become, grounded.

Some Earthy crystals are ★ Jet, Onyx, Aventurine, Magnetite, Emerald, Crysocolla, Smoky Quartz, Malachite and Jadeite.

CRYSTALS & THE AIR ELEMENT

The influence of the Air element may seem less apparent as its effects often occur invisibly, but its nature and essence is very important to some crystals. The most obvious manifestation of Air is in filling spaces, such as bubbles in crystals or the hollows in geodes. Air also provides the elements necessary for chemical reactions to occur during crystal formation. As the element of the intellect, knowledge, mind and clarity, Air symbolically can also fill you with ideas and mental inspiration. Airy crystals can therefore assist in the formulation of concepts and plans, to focus your thoughts and to help you make decisions.

Some Airy crystals are ★ Sapphire, Kunzite, Chalcedony, Turquoise, Lapis Lazuli, Agate, Sodalite, Opal and Rose Quartz.

CRYSTALS & THE WATER ELEMENT

The depositing or the evaporation of Water is a component in the formation of many crystals, including stalagmites and stalactites. Water also finds its balance by assuming its appropriate state as a gas, liquid or solid (ice). Therefore, Water-inspired gemstones help to balance your emotions and influence your dreams by shifting notions between the conscious and unconscious mind.

Some Watery crystals are ★ Pearl, Beryl, Moonstone, Aquamarine, Tourmaline and Amethyst.

CHAPTER FOUR
★
CRYSTALS & THE CHAKRAS

The word 'chakra' comes from the Sanskrit and means 'wheel', disc' or 'circle'. Chakras are vitally important to your physical health, emotional wellbeing and spiritual growth, and are regarded as a complete integrated system that works holistically.

Just as the physical body is pervaded by the nervous system, so the subtle body is pervaded by thousands of channels (*nadi*) through which flow the winds of energy (*prana*). These winds are believed to be vital to our existence and wellbeing. The central channel runs from the crown of the head to the base of the spine and along it are seven focal points known as chakras (*energy wheels*). In most people, just enough energy flows through the chakras to sustain life. However, a specialised practitioner will concentrate on bringing the energy winds together and carrying them along the seven main points, thereby unlocking any emotional or spiritual energy that has been blocked.

The chakras are funnel-shaped spinning energy vortexes of multicoloured light. These swirling vortexes of energy absorb and distribute life-force, the subtle energy known as *prana*.

The seven master chakras - root, sacral, solar plexus, heart, throat, third eye and crown - lie in the centre line of the body, with the first five embedded within the spinal column. Each chakra vibrates at a different vibrational frequency and on a different note.

The first three chakras are connected to individual qualities. The first, called the 'Root Support', at the base of the spine, is linked with security and attachment to the Earth. The second chakra, 'Special Abode', is in the area of the genitals and is concerned with sexual energy and self-confidence. The third chakra is located at the Solar plexus. Known as 'City of the Shining Jewel', it is associated with the achievement of goals, joy and personal power. The fourth chakra, 'Soundless Sound' is located at the heart and holds the power of love and compassion. The fifth chakra, 'Purification', at the throat, is linked with expression, communication and creativity. The last two chakras are connected to realisation and the path to self-actualisation and psychic development. The sixth chakra, 'Command', otherwise known as the Third Eye, is associated with understanding, heightened perception and vision and is located in between the eyebrows. The seventh chakra, the 'Thousand-Petalled Lotus', is the 'Chakra of Great Bliss', said to be opened when one's individual energy and the energy of the cosmos are dissolved and merged into one.

So the lower body chakras deal with physical and survival issues. As we move up the body, the chakras correspond to increasingly spiritual concerns. As a consequence, each chakra's energy vibrates at a different rate, depending on whether they govern earthbound or ethereal issues. The lower chakras have slower and denser vibrations, while the higher chakras spin at faster speeds with higher vibrations.

Each chakra responds to specific life issues or 'thought forms'. The first, or Root Chakra, near the base of the spine, regulates issues of survival and fulfilment of our physical needs for food and shelter. The second, or Sacral Chakra, corresponds to physical desires or appetites. The third, or Solar Plexus Chakra, is connected with issues of power and control. The fourth, or Heart Chakra, deals with matter of love and the heart. The fifth, or Throat Chakra, corresponds to our beliefs, thoughts, and actions involving expression and communication. The sixth, or Third Eye Chakra, governs spiritual sight and clairvoyance. The seventh, or Crown Chakra, lets in universal and Divine knowledge, and is a receiver of wisdom, guidance and understanding.

There are literally hundreds of smaller chakras and they are all interrelated in a very complex system throughout the human body. In addition, other non-physical chakras lie outside the physical body, the best known of which are the Earth Star chakra, located beneath the feet, and the Soul Star chakra, located above the head (higher than the Crown chakra).

Because the chakras have no physical manifestation and cannot be located using any scientific instrument, they have tended to be viewed with scepticism by many Western medical professionals, a distinction they share with energy points in acupuncture and the notion of meridians. Instead, they are believed to have been sensed intuitively by many people over many centuries, and indeed people in yoga positions and in deep meditation have reported experiencing the sensation of a surge of energy rising from the base of the spine and emerging through the top of the head. Some people have even said they have seen points of blue light when their *kundalini* * energy has risen from the lowest chakra to the highest, as well as experiencing a profound sense of happiness and ecstasy.

In summary, the Universal Life Force enters the body through the Crown chakra at the top of the head. As it works its way through the body, it flows through the other centres. As it spreads to the Base chakra, it is said to arouse the kundalini energy, which yogis believe sleeps in a coiled serpentine form.

The Inner Alchemy of the Taoists described the circulation of energies along the central column culminating in the 'Inner Union of Dragon and Tiger'.

The major chakras, the moderators of subtle energy, are envisioned in the Vedas (the primary source of Hindu philosophy) as sacred lotus flowers, with each chakra having lotus with a different number of petals. The seven master chakras are:

ROOT (BASE) ★ Base of Spine ★ Red ★ Earth ★ Security & Survival ★ 4-petalled lotus

SACRAL ★ Below the Navel ★ Orange ★ Water ★ Physical, Sexual, Creative & Material Desires ★ 6-petalled lotus

SOLAR PLEXUS ★ Behind the Navel ★ Yellow ★ Fire ★ Personal Power, Confidence and Control ★ 10-petalled lotus

HEART ★ Heart Region ★ Green ★ Air ★ Love & Compassion ★ 12-petalled lotus

THROAT ★ Throat Region ★ Light Blue ★ Sound/Ether ★ Communication & Self-Expression ★ 16-petalled lotus

THIRD EYE ★ Between the Eyes ★ Dark Blue ★ Light ★ Clairvoyance, Wisdom, Intuition & Vision ★ 2-petalled lotus

CROWN ★ Top of Head ★ Purple ★ Thought/Knowing ★ Spiritual Wisdom & Enlightenment ★ 1000-petalled lotus

* *Kundalini* is a primary energy found at the base of our spine. It is said to look like a coiled snake. In most of us, this serpent power is lying dormant, waiting for our spiritual actualisation. The Tantras, which are spiritual texts on some Hindu, Buddhist and Jain practices, teach that when we begin to work with our spiritual and soul energy system, this force will begin to uncoil and move up through our being, allowing for our primal and most sacred power to unfold, helping us to attain a deep state of enlightenment. On kundalini ★ "She is beautiful like a chain of lightning and fine like a lotus fibre, and shines in the minds of the sages. She is extremely subtle; the awakener of pure knowledge; the embodiment of all bliss, whose true nature is pure consciousness. Shining in her mouth is the *Brahmadvara*. This place ... is sprinkled by ambrosia." - **Sat Cakra Nirupana**

✯ OTHER CHAKRAS TO WORK WITH ✯

As well as the traditional chakras, there are other energy centres that people work with to create an even greater connection to Divine wisdom. These additional chakras are aspects of the self that we can actualise in our spiritual practice. They are:

THE EARTH STAR CHAKRA ★ Found 15 - 30 centimetres below our feet, this chakra is our connection to the Earth and its wisdom and grounding. We can use it to anchor ourselves to the heart of the Earth in order to stabilise ourselves and move in harmony with it. *Gemstones* ~ All black, dark grey, brown & deep red stones.

THE SOUL STAR CHAKRA ★ The soul star, which is seen as a three-dimensional star, is located 15 - 30 centimetres above our crown and we can tap into its energy to awaken deep soul wisdom within us and to access the insights of the cosmos. *Gemstones* ~ Clear Quartz, Diamond, Apophyllite.

THE STELLAR GATEWAY CHAKRA ★ This chakra represents our ability to connect with the Divine cosmos and bring our hopes and dreams into manifestation. It is located around 30 centimetres above the head and is like a vortex that we can enter in order to be suspended in the heart of the Universe. *Gemstones* ~ Clear Quartz, Diamond, Apophyllite, Amethyst.

THE CHAKRAS & ZODIAC CORRESPONDENCES

BASE CHAKRA

The first, the Root or Base chakra, governs and regulates issues of security, survival and fulfilment of our physical needs for food and shelter. It is associated with the zodiac sign of Capricorn.

Location ★ Base of Spine
Colour ★ Red
Concerned with ★ Security & Survival
Gland ★ Gonads
Essential Oils ★ Benzoin, Vetiver, Patchouli
Animals ★ Bull, Elephant, Ox
Shape ★ Yellow Square
Element ★ Earth
Planets ★ Saturn, Earth
Zodiac Sign ★ Capricorn
Flower ★ Four-petalled Lotus
Energy State ★ Solid
Mantra ★ LAM

Positive Expression ★ Energetic, productive, grounded, stable, serves others, committed

Negative Expression (Blockage)★ Angry, self-indulgent, aggressive, plodding, habitual, tied down, prone to anxiety, ungrounded, fearful about security and survival, flighty, difficulty letting go, lack of sense of belonging, weak constitution, overly practical, lacking dreams and imagination

The Base chakra, otherwise known as the Root chakra, is located at the base of the spine. Its Sanskrit name is *muladhara*, and its symbol is a four-petalled crimson lotus flower around a yellow square containing a downward-pointing white triangle. Harmony in this chakra is expressed as groundedness, stability and reliability. When this chakra is balanced you are caring, focused, self-confident, secure, strong and happy, but out of balance it can make you sexually predatory or frigid, manipulative or guilt-ridden. It corresponds to the adrenal glands and the coccygeal nerve plexus. Crystals that can be used to cleanse and balance this chakra are mostly red, black and brown stones, including: Garnet, Fire Agate, Bloodstone, Boji Stone, Red Calcite, Carnelian, Cuprite, Hematite, Brecciated Jasper, Brown Jasper, Red Jasper, Obsidian, Smoky Quartz, Ruby, Black Sapphire, Zircon and Black Tourmaline.

SACRAL CHAKRA

The second, or Sacral chakra, governs sexual, physical, material and creative desires and expressions. It is associated with the zodiac signs of Cancer and Scorpio.

Location ★ Below the Navel
Colour ★ Orange
Concerned with ★ Physical, Sexual, Creative & Material Desires
Gland ★ Cells of Leydig *
Essential Oils ★ Carrot Seed, Dill, Geranium, Jasmine, Hyssop, Neroli, Marjoram, Sandalwood, Rose
Animals ★ Sea Creatures
Shape ★ Light Blue Crescent
Element ★ Water
Planets ★ Moon, Pluto
Zodiac Signs ★ Cancer, Scorpio
Flower ★ Six-petalled Lotus
Energy State ★ Liquid
Mantra ★ VAM

* The Sacral chakra regulates what are called the 'cells of Leydig', which are testicular or ovarian cells that produce and secrete testosterone.

Positive Expression ★ Balanced, creative, personally vital
Negative Expression (Blockage) ★ Imbalanced, over- or undersexed, inflexible, emotionally cold, low energy, low libido, inhibiting, difficulty changing, difficulty experiencing joy, hyper-emotional, overly focused on physical pleasures

The Sacral chakra is located around the sexual organ region. Its Sanskrit name is *svadhisthana*, and its symbol is a six-petalled orange lotus flower containing a second lotus flower and an upward-pointing crescent Moon in a white circle. Balance in this chakra is expressed as originality, creativity and vitality. It corresponds to the sex glands and the sacral nerve plexus. Crystals that can be used to cleanse and balance this chakra are mostly orange stones, including: Carnelian, Amber, Orange Calcite, Citrine, Golden Labradorite (Orange Sunstone), Topaz, Tangerine Quartz and Thulite.

SOLAR PLEXUS CHAKRA

At the root of the navel is the shining lotus of ten petals, of the colour of heavily laden rain clouds. Meditate there on the region of Fire, triangular in form and shining like the rising Sun. outside of it are three Svastika marks, and within, the seed-mantra Ram. By meditating in this manner upon the navel lotus the power to create and destroy the world is acquired.

Sat Cakra Nirupana

The third, or Solar Plexus chakra, governs confidence, personal power and control. It is associated with the zodiac signs of Aries and Leo.

Location ★ Behind the Navel
Colour ★ Yellow
Concerned with ★ Personal Power, Confidence & Control
Gland ★ Adrenals
Essential Oils ★ Chamomile, Neroli, Bergamot, Benzoin, Clary Sage, Dill, Palmarosa,
Cypress, Fennel, Lemon, Hyssop, Juniper, Marjoram, Sage, Black Pepper
Animal ★ Ram
Shape ★ Downward Triangle

Element ★ Fire
Planets ★ Mars, Sun
Zodiac Signs ★ Aries, Leo
Flower ★ 10-petalled Lotus
Energy State ★ Plasma
Mantra ★ RAM

Positive Expression ★ Intelligent, optimistic, forgiving, thoughtful, perceptive
Negative Expression (Blockage)★ Impractical, daydreaming, imbalance between the heart and head, lack of confidence, difficulty manifesting desires, low self-esteem, misuse of power, over-reliance on will, dominance, shame

The Solar Plexus chakra is located at the diaphragm. Its Sanskrit name is *manipura*, and its symbol is a ten-petal yellow lotus flower whose centre contains a red downward-pointing triangle. This is the home of your inner power, a golden, bright sphere of light and pure being. You are able to access your force and strength through this centre. Balance in this chakra is expressed as self-confidence, a feeling of personal empowerment, logical thought processes and goal manifestation. It corresponds to the pancreas and the solar nerve plexus. Crystals that can be used to cleanse and balance this chakra are mostly yellow stones, including: Citrine, Amber, Ametrine, Yellow Jasper, Amblygonite, Golden Beryl, Sunstone, Yellow Sapphire, Tiger's Eye and Yellow Tourmaline.

HEART CHAKRA

The fourth, or Heart chakra, governs all matters of the heart, namely love, openness, wellbeing and compassion. It is associated with the zodiac signs of Libra and Taurus.

Location ★ Heart Region
Colour ★ Green
Concerned with ★ Love & Compassion
Gland ★ Thymus
Essential Oils ★ Clove, Lavender, Lime, Bergamot, Benzoin, Cinnamon, Elemi, Immortelle,
Geranium, Grapefruit, Linden Blossom, Rose, Neroli, Mandarin, Sandalwood, Palmarosa
Animals ★ Antelope, Dove
Shape ★ Hexagram

Element ★ Air
Planet ★ Venus
Zodiac Signs ★ Libra, Taurus
Flower ★ 12-petalled Lotus
Energy State ★ Gas
Mantra ★ YAM

Positive Expression ★ Loving, accepts self and others, innate healer, generous, compassionate
Negative Expression (Blockage) ★ Selfish, envious, jealous, possessive, egotistical, melodramatic, loneliness, lack of emotional fulfilment, difficulty giving or receiving love, lack of compassion, unhealthy relationships, loving too much, unresolved sorrow

The Heart chakra is located in the region of the physical heart. Its Sanskrit name is *anahata*, and its symbol is a twelve-petal green/grey lotus flower whose centre contains a green circle and two intersecting triangles making up a six-pointed star representing balance (six is also the number of Venus, the planetary energy with which the Heart chakra is linked). This chakra blockage is especially significant because it is in the middle, uniting the upper and lower chakras. Among other things, a blockage can manifest as a lack of overall emotional fulfilment and difficulty receiving or being in a state of love. Balance in this chakra is expressed as unconditional love for ourselves and others, as well as openness to give, accept and receive compassion. It corresponds to the thymus and the cardiac nerve plexus. Crystals that can be used to cleanse and balance this chakra are mostly green and pink, such as Rose Quartz, Jade, Green Aventurine, Rhodonite, Watermelon Tourmaline, and Emerald.

THROAT CHAKRA

The fifth, or Throat chakra, governs self-expression, speech and communication, and corresponds to our beliefs, thoughts and actions involving communicating with others. It is associated with the zodiac signs of Gemini and Virgo.

Location ★ Throat Region
Colour ★ Blue
Concerned with ★ Communication, Speech & Self-Expression
Gland ★ Thyroid
Essential Oils ★ Cajeput, Blue Chamomile, Elemi, Cypress, Myrrh, Eucalyptus,

Palmarosa, Ravensara, Black Pepper, Rosemary, Yarrow, Sage
Animals ★ Bull, Elephant, Lion
Shape ★ Downward Triangle
Element ★ Spirit/Ether
Planet ★ Mercury
Zodiac Signs ★ Gemini, Virgo
Flower ★ 16-petalled Lotus
Energy State ★ Vibration
Mantra ★ HAM

Positive Expression ★ Spiritual, self-expressive, willing to work with the Divine, articulate, cooperative, effective communication
Negative Expression (Blockage) ★ Indecisive or wilful, idealistic versus realistic, arrogant, deceptive to self or others, judgemental, problems with self-expression (expression of own truths), inability to communicate ideas or uncontrolled, low-value or inconsistent communication, problems with creativity, manipulative

The Throat chakra is located at the base of the throat. Its Sanskrit name is *vishuddha*, and its symbol is a sixteen-petal blue lotus flower whose centre contains a downward-pointing triangle within which is a circle representing the full Moon. Balance in this chakra is expressed as easy communication with ourselves and others on all levels. It corresponds to the thyroid and parathyroid glands and the pharyngeal nerve plexus. Crystals that can be used to cleanse and balance this chakra are mostly blue stones, including: Blue Lace Agate, Amazonite, Blue Fluorite, Chrysocolla, Blue Chalcedony, Angelite, Aquamarine, Azeztulite, Azurite, Blue Calcite, Larimar ^, Lapis Lazuli, Aqua Aura Quartz, Malachite, Blue Sapphire, Turquoise and Blue Tourmaline. Amber also helps cleanse and balance this area.

^ A rare and powerfully healing gem, larimar is prized by psychics and healers throughout the world.

THIRD EYE CHAKRA

Ajna is like the Moon, beautifully white. It shines with the glory of meditation. Within this lotus dwells the subtle mind. When the yogi ... becomes dissolved in this place, which is the abode of uninterrupted bliss, he then sees sparks of fire distinctly shining.

Sat Cakra Nirupana

The sixth, or Third Eye chakra, governs spiritual sight, Divine connections, intuition, psychic vision, wisdom and clairvoyance. It is associated with the zodiac signs of Sagittarius and Pisces.

Location ★ Between the Physical Eyes
Colour ★ Dark Blue/Indigo
Concerned with ★ Clairvoyance, Wisdom, Intuition & Vision
Gland ★ Pineal
Essential Oils ★ Basil, Angelica Seed, Carrot Seed, Clove Bud, Clary Sage, Ginger, Melissa, Peppermint, Black Pepper
Animal ★ Owl
Shape ★ Downward Triangle
Element ★ Light, Avyakta
Planets ★ Jupiter, Neptune
Zodiac Signs ★ Sagittarius, Pisces
Flower ★ Two-petalled Lotus
Energy State ★ Imagery
Mantra ★ OM

Positive Expression ★ Spiritually wise, intuitive, personal awareness of the Divine
Negative Expression (Blockage)★ Too self-sufficient, lack of imagination, vision or concentration, clouded intuition, inability to see the bigger picture, delusional, distorted imagination or intuition, over-reliance on logic and intellect

The Third Eye chakra is located between and just above the physical eyes. Its Sanskrit name is *ajna*, and its symbol is two large white lotus petals on each side of a white circle, within which is a downward-pointing triangle. This is the home of your intuition or sixth sense; your mind's eye. The purpose of this chakra is to help you to perceive unseen energies such as spirit guides and angels, using your innate clairvoyant, or psychic, skills. You are able to recognise and process spiritual information and wisdom through this centre, as it is connected to your conscious mind also. Balance in this chakra is expressed as developed and sound senses of intuition, clairvoyance, clairaudience and clairsentience. It corresponds to the pituitary gland and the carotid nerve plexus. Crystals that can be used to cleanse and balance this chakra are mostly indigo, deep blue and purple stones such as: Lapis Lazuli, Amethyst, Azurite, Charoite, Lepidolite, Sugilite, Azeztulite, Turquoise, Iolite, Larimar, Blue Calcite, Moldavite, Angelite, Phenacite, Tanzanite and Purple Fluorite.

CROWN CHAKRA

The lotus of the thousand petals, lustrous and whiter than the full Moon, has its head turned downward. It charms. It sheds its rays in profusion and is moist and cool like nectar. The most excellent of men who has controlled his mind and known this place is never again born the Wandering, as there is nothing in the three worlds which binds him.

Sat Cakra Nirupana

The seventh, or Crown chakra, governs spiritual wisdom, higher communication and enlightenment. This is the highest chakra of the seven master chakras and is a receptacle for guidance and understanding from higher 'planes', letting in Universal and Divine knowledge. It is associated with the zodiac sign of Aquarius.

Location ★ Top of Head
Colour ★ Purple, Violet
Concerned with ★ Spiritual Wisdom & Enlightenment
Gland ★ Pituitary
Essential Oils ★ Neroli, Elemi, Violet Wood, Cedarwood, Frankincense, Linden Blossom, Jasmine, Rose, Rosewood
Animals ★ No Animals
Shape ★ Upward Triangle
Element ★ Consciousness/Knowing/Cosmic
Planet ★ Uranus
Zodiac Sign ★ Aquarius
Flower ★ 1,000-petalled Lotus
Energy State ★ Information, Enlightenment

Positive Expression ★ Spiritual, At Oneness, Connectedness, Divine Love
Negative Expression (Blockage) ★ Self-Righteous, spacey, ungrounded, impractical, alienated, indecisive, lack of common sense, difficulty with finishing things, depressed, confused, plagued by a sense of meaninglessness, delusional

The Crown chakra is located just above the crown of the head and does not, therefore have a 'physical' position. Its Sanskrit name is *sahasrara*, and its symbol is the thousand-petal white lotus flower. This is the level of super-consciousness or *samadhi*, a plane beyond time, space and consciousness. Balance in this chakra is expressed as cosmic connection and consciousness. The purpose of this chakra is to keep your soul connected to your angelic body and to All That You Are. You are able to access Divine, Angelic and Spiritual wisdom through this chakra, as it is connected to your higher, astral, and subconscious mind. It corresponds to the pineal gland and the cerebral cortex nerve plexus. Crystals that can be used to cleanse and balance this chakra are clear or violet stones, including: Amethyst, Clear Quartz, Diamond, Angelite, Danburite, Ametrine, Charoite Azeztulite, Lepidolite, Phenacite, Selenite, Tanzanite and Sugilite.

SOME GENERAL SUGGESTIONS FOR LAYOUTS FOR CHAKRA BALANCING *

BASIC / STANDARD

CROWN ★ Amethyst
THIRD EYE ★ Lapis Lazuli
THROAT ★ Blue Lace Agate
HEART ★ Green Aventurine
SOLAR PLEXUS ★ Citrine
SACRAL ★ Carnelian
BASE ★ Red jasper

DYNAMIC

This dynamic layout is powerful and works quickly, using transformative crystals *

CROWN ★ Herkimer Diamond
THIRD EYE ★ Labradorite
THROAT ★ Sapphire
HEART ★ Moldavite
SOLAR PLEXUS ★ Amber
SACRAL ★ Sunstone
BASE ★ Ruby

GENTLE

This layout is more calming and slow in its action *

CROWN ★ Clear Quartz (pointing upwards)
THIRD EYE ★ Iolite
THROAT ★ Turquoise

HEART ★ Green Jade
SOLAR PLEXUS ★ Honey Calcite
SACRAL ★ Carnelian
BASE ★ Red Tiger's Eye

GROUNDING ^ & NURTURING

This is designed to achieve a grounding and peacefully nurturing effect
*

CROWN ★ Amethyst
THIRD EYE ★ Sapphire
THROAT ★ Angelite
HEART ★ Pink and Green Fluorite
SOLAR PLEXUS ★ Amber
SACRAL ★ Carnelian
BASE ★ Hematite

* If you do not have all the crystals listed here, consider others from the same colour group (or from those listed above with their corresponding chakra)

^ *Some Crystals for Grounding:*

BLACK ONYX ★ Protects against negative energy, good for emotional stability; encourages connection to material goals and their achievement.
BLACK TOURMALINE ★ Grounding and protective; absorbs negativity.
HEMATITE ★ Banishes fuzziness and aids concentration, memory and self-discipline; good for self-healing.
JET ★ Grounding, Earth power; wards off nightmares and lifts ill-health.
OBSIDIAN ★ Very powerful grounding stone, reduces escapism and dissolves fear and anger; snowflake obsidian has a softer effect and restores balance and clarity.
SMOKY QUARTZ ★ Lightly grounding and balancing, counteracts hyperactivity, fosters self-acceptance and heightens awareness of Divine protection.

THE MINOR & TRANSPERSONAL CHAKRAS

Most information on the subject of chakras tend to concentrate only on the seven primary chakras, but there are at least four further series of centres processing subtle energies - these are called the minor and transpersonal chakras.

Minor ★ Some minor chakras are located on the palms of the hands and soles of the feet, and there is an immense number along the length of the body's meridians. The classification of chakras into major and minor is an oversimplification. To many, the minor chakras are useful only in a therapeutic context, i.e. for use in acupuncture, reflexology or Reiki for example, and are only taken into account in relation to these therapies. Others are more inclusive. Practitioners of *nei-tan*, or 'internal alchemy', believe that chi, or vital energy, circulates constantly through the body and in this current of energy - the 'circulation of light' or 'microcosmic orbit' - the chakras are junctions. The maintenance of energetic potential and its balance serve only to keep this flowing energy system functioning constantly.

Transpersonal ★ There are four transpersonal chakras: Causal, Star of the Soul and Gateway to the Stars, with one 'inferior' transpersonal chakra, The Star of the Earth.

Causal ★ The Causal chakra is situated at the top of the back of head, around 10 centimetres behind the Crown chakra and links the upper transpersonal chakras to the chain of the seven major chakras

Star of the Soul ★ The Star of the Soul chakra is ethereally situated 15 centimetres above the head and is regarded as a bridge between heaven and Earth, physical and spiritual, essence and reality. It has a great ability to assimilate light. When activated, it is believed to link the energy of the astral plane with physical reality, drawing down the spiritual force of the cosmos via the Causal and Crown chakras.

Gateway to the Stars ★ The Gateway to the Stars chakra is ethereally situated about 30 centimetres above the head and its opening is believed to be the fulfilment of self and has been compared with the most spiritual religious experience. Activated by cosmic rays and by human will focused on a single goal, it is described as a two-way channel that links the person with the cosmos in an authentic mystical experience.

The Star of the Earth ★ The Star of the Earth chakra is considered inferior to the others and is situated about fifteen centimetres below the soles of the feet. While the three 'superior' transpersonal chakras are regarded as uniting people with the Universe - the macrocosm - the Star of the Earth links us with our terrestrial roots. Activating this chakra helps attune the physical body to the regenerative energy of the Earth. None of the upper three transpersonal chakras can be activated unless the Star of the Earth is, too, for there can be no enlightenment without grounding.

AURAS, CHAKRAS & CRYSTALS: A UNITED RELATIONSHIP

An aura or energy field exists around the body of each physical thing; they are energetic extensions of the body, consisting of very fine electromagnetic energy. The electromagnetic vibrations emitted by the three layers of light that compose the aura can be sensed up to three or four metres away from the body, according to auric therapists. They develop their maximum strength at a distance of between seven and 40 centimetres.

Our auras are composed of seven layers. The densest layer is the etheric body, which lies next to our physical body. The next, extending out in order, are the Emotional Body, Mental Body, Astral Layer, Etheric Template, Celestial Body and Ketheric Template.

Contact with these energy fields produces an interaction of energy to which the vibrations emitted by crystals may bring balance and wellbeing. The aura forms an oval of light which is made up of three layers, representing our invisible selves: the ethereal or energetic, the emotional or astral, and the mental. Our auras become balanced or unbalanced on contact with the aura of another body, depending on the energy given off by it.

The ethereal (energetic) aura's function is to preserve the energy of our bodies and nourish it with energy captured from the cosmos or from other physical bodies such as minerals or crystals. The emotional (astral) aura's function is to concentrate the emotional energy of the body and communicate it to the physical aura. The mental aura's function is to control and balance the interaction between the ethereal and emotional auras; it contains the templates for our understanding of reality and our beliefs and behaviour.

The great majority of people cannot see the aura with the naked eye, but it is believed to be possible to train certain natural, but often undeveloped, forms of perception to become aware of the aura. An easier approach is Kirlian photography, which can capture an image of the usually invisible aura surrounding a body. Science rejected the idea of the aura for a long time, until the mid-20th century, when Russian scientist Semyon Kirlian used a new photographic technique, took an image of his hand and found that it was surrounded by a luminous field of coloured light. This was the first photograph of the phenomenon.

Each of us has a predominant colour in our aura, although other colours may come and go according to our state of health and our emotions. The main colours in one's aura and their basic meanings and corresponding chakras are:

Colour	Meaning	Chakra
Red	Energy, survival, drive, action, leadership, innovation	Base
Orange	Optimism, confidence, emotional warmth, sensuality	Sacral
Yellow	Communication, creativity, gregariousness, mental agility, power	Solar Plexus
Green	Love, kindness, peace, compassion, love of nature, need for harmony	Heart
Pink	Affection, compassion, comfort, strong spirituality	Heart
Blue	Consideration, idealism, ethical values, expression, communication	Throat
Indigo/Purple	Love, psychic ability, spiritual purpose, intuition, clairvoyance	Third Eye
White	Spiritual evolution, humanitarianism, self-actualisation, wisdom, connection with the Divine & the Cosmos	Crown

CHAPTER FIVE
★
CRYSTALS & THEIR MEANINGS

★ AGATE ★

Agate reminds us that no matter the base material we start with, it can be tempered and transformed by spiritual alchemy.

Judy Hall

Main Spiritual & Metaphysical Qualities ★ Connects one with one's inner self; cleansing; soothing; balancing; calming; transmutes dark emotions into positive ones; helps during difficult or challenging life situations; promotes self-acceptance & forgiveness.

Astrological Affinities ★ Most zodiac signs, depending on type. Gemini, Virgo, Mercury

Magical Tips ★ Agate increases receptivity to spiritual currents. Wear it and touch it frequently to help connect you to these currents & to give you strength.

Vibration ★ Earthy

Agates are a kind of chalcedony belonging to the quartz family, and come in a variety of colours and patterns, each with its own special qualities. But all agates are protective and nurture natural talents and relationships, acting as shields to protect you on your spiritual journey.

Since the times of Ancient Babylon and Ancient Greece, in which it was sacred to the Greek god of healing Aesclepius, agate has been used as a charm of healing and protection. Agate was one of the first stones to be used by humans, with worked pieces dating back to 25,000 BC.

Agate has concentric layers made up of quartz and opal fibres, giving it its often streaky, dual-toned appearance. Some of its vast array of colours are: blue, brown, red (blood agate), green, orange, yellow and white. The therapeutic properties of agates are linked to their colours, which vary widely according to the different minerals they contain.

The Ancient Egyptians favoured varieties with white bands, as they associated this with purification and clarity. Today, banded agate is believed to possess great receptive and intuitive energies. This type of agate, which combines the qualities of the Earth element (the dark tones) to the Moon element (its white bands), is said to strengthen creativity and spirituality. It is also believed to promote a sense of calm and balance when used in meditation. Banded agate varieties are said to help increase self-esteem, increase receptive and intuitive energies, improve willpower, promote calm, and stimulates creativity and spirituality.

Agate tunes and strengthens the body and mind and imparts a sense of strength and courage. Its power comes from its ability to promote circulation of energy around the body. It helps to induce a peaceful and calming atmosphere, making it especially useful for various types of mind/body/spirit healers and therapists.

Agate helps to keep words and thoughts in good order by keeping you truthful and genuine; it facilitates the ability to discern the truth and accept circumstances. Some types of agate are beneficial for establishing boundaries and keeping negative influences or people outside your auric field.

It is a wonderful stone to use during pregnancy because it soothes, balances, and calms both mother and baby throughout gestation and labour. Additionally, it can enhance sleep quality, soothe angry feelings, enhance communication, neutralise aggression, and encourage clearer thinking.

Grounding yet energetic, all agates possess powerful healing properties.

★ AGATE ~ BLUE LACE ★

Main Spiritual & Metaphysical Qualities ★ Balances emotions; instils peace of mind; eases depression, fear & hysteria; promotes calm & a sense of wellbeing; unblocks thoughts & expression; encourages one to speak one's truth; improves ability to communicate & concentrate.

Astrological Affinities ★ Sagittarius, Aquarius, Pisces

Magical Tips ★ Blue lace agate is believed to endow its wearer with grace and the persuasive power of speech. Philosopher Bernard Mandeville said of it: "It makes one a beautiful speaker and gracious with words ... and helps one to acquire intelligence and sense." If you have an important public speech to make, or wish to convey an important message to others, try using blue lace agate as your ally. Wear blue lace agate near your Throat chakra to open up the voicing of your most profound personal and spiritual truths.

Blue lace agate is a soft, sky-blue, opaque gemstone which displays its innocent purity and gentle character in translucent, white lacy patterns. It is an effective healing stone and its soft energy is cooling and quietening, bringing peace of mind, nurturance and support to its carrier or wearer. It is an excellent calming stone to place in a meditation or healing space to enhance the atmosphere. It can also be used in meditative 'journeys' to expand the mind into new realms or to help dissolve worries and cares and taken as a 'gem essence' can bring a sense of peace and calm to the whole system, especially in cases of emotional trauma or severe anxiety.

Blue lace agate can alleviate suppressed or repressed memories, encouraging their expression and dissolving old patterns. For males, it is useful in helping them get more in touch with their sensitive, yin feeling natures.

Spiritually, blue lace agate can link thoughts to a more spiritual vibration and clears the Throat chakra so that one's highest spiritual truths can be expressed. In fact, it is a powerful throat healer, both physically and spiritually, so is most effective if worn around this area.

It also balances the Heart, Third Eye and Crown chakras. Overall, this soft-toned crystal encourages patience, kindness, peace, honesty and wisdom, and calms and strengthens one's spiritual centre.

★ ALEXANDRITE ★

Main Spiritual & Metaphysical Qualities ★ Regenerative; renewing; improves memory; aids in spiritual transformation; protective; encourages joy & bliss.

Astrological Affinities ★ Gemini, Virgo

Magical Tips ★ A notable feature of this crystal is its stunning optical property of colour change - it is light red or red-purple in incandescent artificial light, and green (often an intense grass-green) or blue-green in daylight. Since green is the colour of new growth and pink the shade of impartial love, the Russian name for Alexandrite, 'Stone of Good Omen', could not be more apt. This stone has a positive electrical charge which stays for hours after rubbing, and an energy factor which changes with its colour.

Vibration ★ High

Alexandrite is a variety of chrysoberyl, a beryllium aluminium oxide with a hardness of 8.5. One of the hardest gemstones, second only to diamond and corundum, alexandrite is an enchanting crystal carrying powerful properties. It opens the intuition and metaphysical abilities and creates a strong will and personal magnetism. It carries a very joyful vibration and is a powerful agent of inner transformation and spiritual evolution.

One of the world's rarest gemstones, the finest specimens of alexandrite are more costly than diamonds - and its price understandably reflects its rarity. Discovered in the Ural Mountains of Russia in around 1830 on the birthday of Czar Alexander II and named after him, its key words are joy, wisdom and the release of sorrow. Depending on lighting, alexandrite can display colours of light red to blue-green. This is a stone of contrasts; for potent though this stone appears, it radiates sensitivity. In physical healing, it bypasses the actual condition and goes directly to the root of it and balances any disharmonies out. It is a regenerative stone, aiding the tissues of the body to renew after dis-ease - both internally and externally. It has even been used to treat leukaemia and cancer. These regenerative properties also extend to spiritual transformation and growth, enhancing your ability to find joy in life and aiding psychic protection when undertaking such work. It also carries the beneficial qualities of making one's head feel 'roomier', improving the memory, clearing the eyesight, and relieving any physical tensions.

In its notable colour changes, alexandrite signifies a spiritual metamorphosis and embodies an inner pattern of flexibility, adaptability and willingness to shift its expression in the presence of varying conditions; it can teach us this very quality in ourselves.

Since its discovery, alexandrite was believed to be a stone of good fortune in its native country. Primarily stimulating the Crown chakra, it embodies both the heart energy (green) and the higher mind energy (purple). It can stimulate a harmonic opening of the Heart, Third Eye and Crown chakras, during which the three can operate as an integrated whole.

Alexandrite's emotional tone is one of exuberant joy. It calls forth the heart's natural state of delighted engagement and teaches us that the spiritual qualities of the celestial realms are also simultaneously here at every moment, encouraging us to take on all the energies that come to us and to do this with a pure commitment to bliss.

Overall, it centres, reinforces and realigns the mental, emotional and spiritual bodies, enhancing manifestation in all its forms. This precious, rare gem transmits inner peace by developing magnanimity of heart and should be valued and used extensively - if you are lucky enough to find one!

★ AMAZONITE ★

Main Spiritual & Metaphysical Qualities ★ Combats anxiety & stress; improves communication both with your inner & outer world; balances yin & yang; transmutes destructive emotional patterns; helps one to create a new reality through creative thinking; attracts friendship; stimulates the will to live; aids with self-understanding; filters electromagnetic pollution; helps connect you to your soul group; promotes strength & fortitude; magnetises luck & good fortune.

Astrological Affinities ★ Venus, Taurus, Virgo, Libra

Magical Tips ★ Traditionally, amazonite was highly prized by gamblers, who were said to find it effective at attracting luck in games of chance. This quality is linked to amazonite's reputed ability to help you attain success in any objective you set yourself. It has been used by those wishing to ensure business success and by shamans to attract good fortune.

Vibration ★ Earthy

An opaque, blue-green feldspar, this stone's nickname is the 'hope stone', and it is considered a new age gem. Also known as Amazon stone, it has a fine, characteristic brilliant blue-green colour.

Its name is believed to have come from the mythical race of female warriors who were said to give the stone to men who visited them. Greek mythology told of this matriarchal tribe of women warriors who worshipped Artemis, goddess of the hunt, wild regions, and the Moon. The Greeks believed these women, the Amazons, inhabited a mystical place somewhere between the known and unknown worlds.

Due to its fine and attractive shade of green, amazonite has long been used in jewellery.

Amazonite appropriates self-love like rose quartz, but on a more intimate as well as multi-dimensional level. Indeed, it encourages faith in both the Divine and in the Self.

Amazonite aids perseverance, fights against exhaustion, and allows you to discover and tap into the personal powers that already exist within you. Its key word is balance: it is believed to balance masculine and feminine energies, align the physical and ethereal bodies, and calm the nervous system. Amazonite can be held in meditation to take you beyond yourself, alleviating any fears of out-of-body experiences.

Amazonite can be useful for someone who is terminally ill - having it in the room can ease their transition into the next realm.

An active gem, amazonite is believed to reinforce the vitality of the individual and stimulate the will to live. Excellent for enhancing creativity and lifting self-esteem, amazonite also provides a sense of continuity between mind, body and spirit. Amazonite encourages a belief in one's Self and on a psychic level, it aligns the physical, astral and etheric bodies, making astral travel easier and coming back smoother.

★ AMBER ★

Pretty, in amber to observe the forms,
Of hairs, or straws, or dirt, or grubs, or worms!
The things, we know, are neither rich nor rare,
But wonder how the devil they got there.

Pope

Main Spiritual & Metaphysical Qualities ★ Protective; renewing; transmutes negative energies into positive ones; cleanses & re-activates the chakras; motivating; aid in decision-making; promotes trust, peacefulness & altruism; instils energy, courage & personal power.

Astrological Affinities ★ The Sun, Cancer, Leo, Scorpio, Capricorn, Aquarius

Magical Tips ★ Pliny, a first century Roman author, naturalist and philosopher, believed that amber was created by moisture from the rays of the Sun falling to Earth, and it was therefore associated with the Sun's renewing and life-giving energy. Those who have a strong Solar influence in their natal chart can use amber to channel this energy to create magic in their inner and outer lives. Its associations with the Sun make it a great conductor of success, abundance, healing, joy and vitality. A powerful stone for manifestation, it is also said to be a powerful attractor of one's Soul Mate. In alchemy Amber is a synonym for gold and was prized in ancient times. This pale yellow resin exuded by various trees (pine, fir, poplar, alder) was closely linked by the alchemists to both gold and the Sun (Sol). It was regarded by many as a type of 'vegetable gold'.

Vibration ★ Earthy

Though not actually a stone - it is fossilised tree resin from an extinct form of pine that was submerged under the ocean many millions of years ago - amber is a powerful material to work with. It is one of the oldest substances used for jewellery, will attract pieces of paper when rubbed, and can generate an electrical charge when rubbed against cloth; many associate it with purely charged power for this reason. It is therefore effective in giving an extra energetic boost to any magical workings you may undertake, such as spells, ceremonies and rituals. With its reputation of being effective at storing magical charge, it can be charged up and carried or worn as a talisman to attract more positive energy in areas such as love, success or luck.

Amber has been celebrated in many ancient cultures as a bringer of courage and honesty and in China it was known as the 'Soul of the Tiger' and even thought to protect against fire and water. In Ancient Rome, amber was given to gladiators for courage.

Though it has been used by humans since the Stone Age, jewellery made from it has become increasingly popular in recent years. One common use for amber jewellery is that of baby adornments, which are widely believed to alleviate the pain and discomfort of teething. The theory is that the child's body heats the amber, which in turn releases oils containing trace amounts of succinic acid. This acid then gets absorbed into the bloodstream where the compound acts as a natural analgesic and anti-inflammatory, reducing swelling as well as easing the baby's pain.

Amber may be transparent or translucent and has a greasy shine and sometimes cloudy appearance. As well as its well-known yellow, orange or reddish-brown colour, amber is found in a range of other colours, including black, violet, blue, green and white (bone amber). Amber with a cloudy appearance due to internal bubbles is known as bastard amber. Blue and green colouration can form when amber contains trapped air bubbles, which cause a fluorescent light effect. Reddish-hued specimens are known as ruby amber. Popular jewellery amber is often a beautiful dewy golden honey colour.

Some types are also named after their place of origin, such as bacalite (Baja California, Mexico), burmite (Myanmar, formerly Burma) and roumanite (Romania), the most common being succinite, found in the Baltic, sometimes referred to as 'true amber'.

Over the centuries, philosophers and alchemists conjured up delightful but fanciful theories to explain the origins of this intriguing millions-of-years-old resin, with its trapped insects, pieces of moss, spider webs, feathers, eggs, reptiles, lichens and pine needles forever frozen in time. This honey-like crypt for all manner of prehistoric life forms, makes amber a peculiar and unique material, and it is believed that it is unlikely to exist on any other planet but Earth.

On a metaphysical and spiritual level, amber can be used to boost your energy and courage, to enhance powers of recall, and even to improve your finances. If you suffer from timidity and a fear of speaking your mind, it can instil bravery, inner strength and confidence.

Also connected to the Sun due to its colouring, amber is often used in wealth spells; this may also be a legacy of ancient times when only the wealthy could afford to wear this enchanting material. Amber has uplifting energies, helps you to find humour and joy, alleviates stress, aids spiritual expansion, is especially beneficial for people suffering depression or suicidal thoughts, and helpful if you are feeling weighed down with responsibilities. It also has a positive effect when you are feeling powerless or out of control, reminding you of your inner strength and personal achievements.

Worn as jewellery, amber can be grounding and stabilising. When used on the Solar Plexus, with which it most resonates, it can enhance clarity about your future path or purpose. When used on the Sacral chakra, with which is also has a strong affinity, it promotes sensuality, emotional and sexual connection, and helps to stimulate physical, sexual, creative and material desires.

Amber rapidly heals gaps, tears, holes and other wounds in the aura caused by emotional imbalances; it also provides protection against other people's negative energies which may cause auric damage.

Overall, amber is a powerful healer and cleanser that absorbs negative energies and transmutes them into positive forces which facilitate deep healing within the body and psyche. Still believed to bestow joy, spontaneity, purification of body, mind and spirit, confidence, and good luck, it seems that time has not diminished our belief in amber as a potent healer.

★ AMETHYST ★

The 'house of the gods' is the ninth celestial house and naturally the sign Sagittarius. The giving of prosperity is ever an attribute of Jupiter, and the measure and the source of the gift are shown in the nativity or map of the heavens at a person's birth. The ancients connected the amethyst with the ninth celestial mansion - the mansion of Sagittarius.

Isidore Kozminsky

The Spiritual Stone

Main Spiritual & Metaphysical Qualities ★ Calms the spirit; increases spiritual & intuitive faculties; raises psychic awareness; urges the highest ideals and truths; aids stability; encourages inner peace; good for meditation; protects the energy field (aura); attracts good luck; relieves insomnia.

Astrological Affinities ★ Jupiter, Neptune, Sagittarius, Capricorn, Aquarius Pisces

Magical Tip ★ Keep unpolished amethyst near other crystals to charge them. Amethyst aligns & activates the Third Eye, Crown, Soma, Soul Star and Stellar Gateway chakras, helping one to connect to an exceptionally high level of cosmic connection and consciousness. Amethyst is well-known for opening the Third Eye and thereby clarifying one's spiritual vision.

Vibration ★ High

An extremely well-known, common, easy-to-source and popular stone, amethyst is the stone of spiritual power and psychic energy. It encompasses power, spirit, beauty, serenity, healing, and magic. Amethyst's name is derived from the Greek word *amethystos*, literally meaning "not intoxicated." Its violet colour is created by the presence of iron oxide impurities in its crystals.

Its colour varies from pale lilac to an intense purple, depending on its iron content. The lighter shade of amethyst is aligned with Jupiter - the planet of spiritual expansion, whereas the darker variety is associated with Pluto - the planet of spiritual transformation. In general, amethyst's purple colour is related to all forms of transcendence, and when worn this crystal can activate the lymphatic system, strengthen the nervous system, and protect the energy field of its wearer.

Amethyst is a 'soul direction stone', which means that the 'soul' purpose of the wearer can be aligned with the crystal. A rough or cut piece placed in a meditation area can also help to foster a strong field of meditative energy.

Many people are attracted to wearing the beautiful amethyst crystal in jewellery. Amethyst, like all quartz crystals, can be worn and used in conjunction with all other gems. You can place a crystal on a piece of amethyst or other quartz to clean and recharge it, as well as to augment the various properties of the gemstone needing a boost.

Connected with the Crown and Third Eye Chakras, this beautiful purple stone is used to aid and promote spiritual wisdom, intuition, protection, focus, inner peace, pleasant dreams, meditation, spiritual awareness, psychic abilities, and overall healing. Calming, balancing and comforting, amethyst is a stone commonly used and worn by healers and spiritual workers, as it has the power to focus energies, brings forth 'unseen' realms, and heightens one's psychic perceptions. Indeed, its best known use is for heightening and enhancing one's spiritual connections and insights; it can even open doors to other dimensions, planes and realities. Many spiritualists believe that it can also bring the Divine into the mundane parts of your life, heighten your receptivity to all manner of things, and generally enhance *all* healing.

This charming stone awakens and activates our higher awareness and psychic abilities and has been used since biblical times; it is mentioned in Exodus as one of the 12 sacred stones worn on the High Priest Aaron's breastplate. Purple has long been considered a royal colour, so it is not surprising that amethyst has been so revered and so much in demand throughout history. Amethysts are featured in the English Crown Jewels and were also a favourite of Ancient Egyptian royalty. The Ancient Egyptians consecrated it as a stone to the god of wisdom, Thoth, while in Ancient Greece it was associated with

Mercury. Enchanted by the stone's energy, Leonardo da Vinci wrote that amethyst could dissipate evil thoughts and quicken the intelligence.

Amethyst has a high ethereal vibration and is an extremely powerful, healing and protective stone, particularly for those born in February and under the signs of Aquarius and Pisces; indeed, it is the sacred birthstone for the month of February.

Amethyst has strong cleansing and healing powers, and its serenity assists with enhancing meditation and the reaching of higher states of consciousness. It fights against inferiority complexes, insecurities and fears, through calming states of stress.

Connected with the Crown and Third Eye chakras, amethyst offers protection, wisdom, focus, power, access to Divine understanding, ethereal awareness, and increases psychic abilities, healing and inner peace. The radiation of violet light issuing from amethyst has been placed on record as providing a calming influence upon the nerves, making it balancing and comforting to the wearer, and is said to be instrumental in slowing rapid and agitated bodily movements, and helpful in easing neuralgia, headaches, gout and stress-related insomnia.

Amethyst can be worn on parts of the upper body to encourage conversations with your higher self, and is especially beneficial when worn over the throat or heart. Encouraging selflessness, intuition, spiritual wisdom and Divine visualisation, amethyst can transmute earthly energies to the higher vibrations of etheric realms. As a stone of tranquillity and contentment, it can also dispel anger, irritability, mood swings, fear and negativity. Amethyst can act as a compassionate anchor and ensures that you are emitting your energy from a place of peace and understanding.

Amethyst is extremely beneficial in all crystal therapy and healing work. When placed in a therapy room, an amethyst quartz cluster will emit a powerful purifying energy, facilitating healing in both the practitioner and the individual undergoing treatment. An amethyst geode or cluster infuses an area with tranquillity and eases the immediate environment's geopathic stress and electromagnetic vibrations.

Known as 'the spiritual stone', amethyst is one of the most powerfully psychic, healing and calming crystals that you can work with.

★ ANGELITE ★

Main Spiritual & Metaphysical Qualities ★ Promotes serenity; calms the mind; alleviates fear & anger; encourages forgiveness, communication & truth; facilitates communication with angels.

Astrological Affinities ★ Taurus, Libra, Venus

Magical Tips ★ Angelite can be used to open up Divine channels, to enable communication with your guardian angels, spirit guides, and Higher Self.

Angelite is an alluring and gentle pale blue stone that promotes serenity, inner peace and a sense of calm. It is commonly known as an angelic connection stone, hence its name, and psychically it can enhance astral travel, telepathy, psychic awareness, and spirit journeys. As a Throat chakra stone, it is an excellent tonic for communication, and uncovering and speaking one's Truth.

★ APOPHYLLITE ★

Main Spiritual & Metaphysical Qualities ★ Promotes high levels of self-awareness; restorative; calms the mind; gently brings the truth to the surface; brings illumination & clarity to situations; self-attunement; removes confusion; promotes honesty & harmony with others.

Astrological Affinities ★ Gemini, Libra

Magical Tips ★ When placed on the Third Eye, Apophyllite can be used to enhance one's metaphysical abilities, such as telepathy and clairvoyance. Apophyllite allows you access to the Akashic Record so you can read the cosmic account of your future or facilitate karmic healing of past issues.

Vibration ★ Exceptionally High

Apophyllite creates a conscious connection between the physical and spiritual realms. It helps one recognise and act upon the Truth in all situations. Through using apophyllite in mediation, this Truth will rise gently to the surface so that imbalances can be resolved and your soul's karmic peace can be restored. It can be used to open the Third Eye and to bring light and energy into the Heart chakra.

★ AQUAMARINE ★

Gem-quality aquamarine is found above 14,000 feet on Mount Antero in the Rocky Mountains ... Only the hardiest souls venture into the rugged slopes of this temperamental mountain - a fitting metaphor for a stone believed to summon the spirits of light to counteract the forces of darkness and assist the soul on its journey to enlightenment.

Judy Hall

Main Spiritual & Metaphysical Qualities ★ Eliminates fear; sharpens mental perception; inspires hope in the heart; refines the intuition; removes discordant vibrations; promotes creative expression & harmonious communication; soothes emotions; enhances spirituality; supportive & reassuring during difficult life situations.

Astrological Affinities ★ Aries, Taurus, Gemini, Libra, Scorpio, Aquarius, Pisces, The Moon, Venus, Uranus, Water Element

Magical Tips ★ Wearing an aquamarine close to your Heart chakra can help attract love of all kinds.

Vibration ★ High

This hard gemstone, which forms in long hexagonal crystals, is a pale blue-green variety of a mineral type called beryl, a group which also includes emeralds. True aquamarine has a translucent pale turquoise colour. The energy of our body's life force is sky-blue, which is the same colour the earth is perceived as when seen from space, and it is also the same hue as the tint reflected in the blue of the aquamarine.

Aquamarine's name suggests its link to the enchanting water kingdom - *aqua* is Latin for water, and *marine* means 'of the sea'. It is a vital tool in cleansing and purifying the 'water element' of our psyches, a symbol of our emotions and feelings. Our bodies being over 70 per cent in watery make-up, keeping this element balanced is crucial to our wellbeing. Ultimately, aquamarine helps to cleanse the water element deep within ourselves, clearing away emotional toxicity and bringing inner peace. Its energy indeed is that of water - flowing but strong, gentle and compassionate, moving around obstacles with ease.

Aquamarine has been believed to bring good luck to lovers since the time of the Ancient Greeks and Romans. It is said to attract and maintain good fortune and love if worn or carried; its talismanic powers can be recharged by leaving it under a Full Moon and sprinkling it the next morning with water left overnight in the same moonlight.

Aquamarine works on the Sacral and Throat chakras and helps open you up to love by removing blockages and balancing the sexual urges against other qualities that attract you to another, leaving you more receptive to love and its influence.

Many crystal practitioners, knowing this gem's healing value, may work through an aquamarine to examine a person's surrounding life-force, which manifests itself to those sensitive enough to see them in billions of fine, hair-like blue arrows. If the practitioner assesses this radiating energy to be steady and of consistent strength throughout its flow, then all is well in the subject's energy field. If however, it is seen to be inconsistent or to thin out here or there, then physical strength may be on the wane - this condition may or may not be healable, but the significant factor here is that it is detectable.

Aquamarine once bore the title 'All Life' and is a gem that must be listened to, not ordered about; its powers will depend upon its user's receptiveness and it will work on the level that he or she is able to achieve.

An effective balm for swollen feet and a soother of frayed emotions and nerves, aquamarine refines the faculties of the intuitive mind and removes discordant vibrations. Aquamarine shields the aura and aligns the chakras, and is also an excellent crystal to boost, stimulate, activate and cleanse the Throat chakra, enhancing immunity and keeping the bridge clear between the Heart and the Throat chakras.

This enchanting gem encourages creative verbal expression and harmonious communications, clears up confusion, sharpens intuition, opens up the pathways for clairvoyance, invokes spiritual consciousness, endows us with courage, and alleviates powerful unpleasant feelings such as grief, despair and loneliness.

It will enable you to find deeper satisfaction when you are feeling discouraged or empty, being reassuring, uplifting and pointing the way towards spiritual fulfilment. It also helps in situations where you need to be or feel in control, imparting feelings of inspiration, calmness, peace, love and 'flow'. It promotes the courage to express one's self truthfully and openly, and is useful in helping one release self-defeating patterns, destructive habits, self-pity or a victim mentality.

★ AVENTURINE ★

Main Spiritual & Metaphysical Qualities ★ A versatile healing stone; helps one overcome a 'poverty consciousness'; brings joy & abundance; increases confidence.

Astrological Affinities ★ Aries, Taurus, Cancer, Libra

Magical Tips ★ Adventuring is said to have a powerful connection to the devic * kingdom.

Vibration ★ Earthy to High, depending on colour

Aventurine is a notably brilliant form of cryptocrystalline quartz. Coming in hues of green, blue, yellow, red, pink and glowing sunset, aventurine is a unique member of the quartz family and owes its fine gold-speckled appearance to tiny flakes of green fuchsite (a form of mica with added chrome), mica or hematite in its body.

This gem is identified with the stone called by Pliny the "Sandaresus: of stars of gold gleaming from within."

It is said that the name aventurine (*per aventura*, by chance or accident) arose from an accident in a Venetian glass factory, where a workman found that eight parts of ground glass, one part protoxide of copper and two parts of iron oxide well-heated and allowed to cool slowly, produced the peculiar appearance admired in the real gem to even better effect. This seemingly alchemical creation was called goldstone (see *Goldstone*).

* The term 'devic' relates to the kingdom of the devas, or nature spirits, believed to inhabit or reign over natural objects such as trees, mountains or bodies of water. People with clairvoyance are sometimes able to see or communicate with these spirits, by gaining intuitive access to the device kingdom, the energetic level at which these entities exist.

★ AVENTURINE ~ GREEN ★

Main Spiritual & Metaphysical Qualities ★ Strengthens capacity for personal growth; enhances sentimental relations; inspires artistic expression; facilitates verbal expression; assists with luck; eases insomnia & other sleep disturbances; helps with new ideas & change; increases the ability to think creatively; assists freedom to pursue new ideas; enhances the ability to sustain changes.

Astrological Affinities ★ Taurus, Libra

Magical Tips ★ Green aventurine is sometimes called 'fairy treasure' and is said to be the luckiest of all crystals. Keep one with you in a green bag and a four-leaved clover if you can get one, for all games of chance. Green amazonite in the same bag will increase the luck and magnetism.

Place three in a dish in front of your garden gnome to attract good luck into your home.

Vibration ★ Earthy

Green is aventurine's most common colouring and this variety is considered the 'opportunity, chance and luck stone'. Legend has it that a seventeenth century Venetian glass-blower was working with some green molten glass when he inadvertently let copper fillings fall onto it. It had a most striking colour and he called it aventurina, from the Italian *a ventura*, which literally means 'by accident'. When natural coloured quartzes with similar appearance were discovered later, they were given the same name.

Because aventurine's name is derived from the Italian for 'chance' or 'random', it is believed to help us to recognise opportunities. It is said to place us exactly where we need to be for good things to transpire, as energetically it opens our mind to increased perception and creative insights, so that we are better able to recognise favourable circumstances.

Connected with the Heart chakra, green aventurine helps activate, clear and protect the heart, and is generally useful for treating heart problems on account of its ability to strengthen and stabilise the heart, as well as encourage regeneration of this vital organ - both physically and emotionally. A stone of comfort, balance and tranquillity, green aventurine is favoured by healers who wish to promote wholeness and harmony.

Aventurine encourages leadership, decisiveness, compassion, empathy, creativity and perseverance, and defuses negative situations and emotions. It also promotes new growth, optimism, and is an attractor of luck, wealth and prosperity - it is a traditional gambler's talisman. Aventurine has long enjoyed a reputation as a powerful manifestor of abundance; it works by drawing the energising strength of the Sun down to Earth to power this manifestation and attract prosperity.

Aventurine is a stone of comfort and balance, encourages regeneration, and opens the heart and restores trust, so is an excellent stone for those who find it difficult to open up their hearts to giving and receiving love. It is a powerful tonic and curative for all kinds of emotional disturbances, including stress, anxiety, fears, depression or psychological apparitions that affect the equilibrium of character and behaviour. It emits the greatest vibrations of the four opaque quartzes used in gem therapy, making aventurine a useful agent in maintaining harmony between the physical and the emotional; many crystal therapists recommend it for those who suffer from manias, phobias and compulsions.

Green aventurine will assist you to move on from a limited vision of your capabilities, and, encouraging exploration, it is helpful in career assessment or changes.

Overall, aventurine, and particularly green aventurine, is an all-round healer, stimulating wellbeing, joy, good fortune and abundance, and enables you to live within your own centre.

★ AVENTURINE ~ RED ★

Main Spiritual & Metaphysical Qualities ★ Relieves timidity & fears; increases energy, vitality & enthusiasm; enhances creativity; restores good humour; protects against environmental pollution.

Astrological Affinities ★ Aries, Scorpio

Magical Tips ★ Red aventurine is believed to bring money when carried in a small red bag with a sprinkling of spice such as cinnamon or ginger. It is said to attract good luck when the odds are against you - hold a small crystal, call out your need, then throw it as far as possible; the finder will be lucky too!

Vibration ★ Earthy to High

Aventurine's characteristic feature is the inclusion of sparkling grains of crystalline mica. Light reflecting from these inclusions generates a spangling effect known as 'aventurinment'. In red aventurine, this effect results from the presence of brown mica and red hematite, which gives this stone a dark reddish cast.

Red aventurine helps to combat fear and insecurities, and prevents us from falling into despair. Its energising properties strengthen one's vitality and being connected with the Base and Sacral chakras, it can stimulate and attune our sensual desires.

Its vibrations are believed to enhance creative abilities, awaken the desire to begin new things, and helps to combat shyness, allowing us to explore new sensations and territories where fear has previously held us back.

★ AZURITE ★

Main Spiritual & Metaphysical Qualities ★ Attunes one to spiritual guidance & evolution; increases focus & receptivity to vibrations; healing; insightful; transformative; alleviates negative feeling states.

Astrological Affinities ★ Taurus, Sagittarius, Capricorn, Aquarius, Mercury

Magical Tips ★ Azurite has the peculiar quality of slowly but inexorably morphing from royal blue and into another mineral, the deep green malachite. During its working life as azurite, however, it frees channels along which its wearers might fear to tread. As malachite, this stone has physical healing properties as well as emotional. But as azurite, it seems to operate almost entirely on the spiritual level alone.

Vibration ★ High

Azurite is a deep royal blue mineral which occurs in small crystals or spherical balls. Azurite was regarded as a sacred stone by the Native Americans, who believed that it facilitated contact with their spirit guides. The Ancient Chinese called azurite the stone of heaven because they believed it opened celestial gateways. The Mayans used this stone to heighten their psychic powers, as well as to transfer knowledge and wisdom via the medium of thought and communication.

Azurite is particularly beneficial for the Throat and Third Eye chakras and is often called the 'stone of heaven'. Azurite guides psychic and intuitive development and urges the soul toward enlightenment. It stimulates the Third Eye chakra, raising consciousness to a higher level and attuning one to spiritual guidance and unfoldment.

Azurite is a vision stone that assists by helping the mind release surrounding chaos and noise which is preventing one from being fully present and effective. It increases focus and sensitivity and allows the higher mind to receive finer vibrations.

A powerful healing stone, azurite facilitates entering a mediative state, and enhances the understanding of any psychosomatic origins behind dis-ease within us (the effect of the mind and emotions on the physical body). Azurite allows us to reach deeper insights by expanding the mind and opening one up to new perspectives. It inspires the mind and is useful in meditation, helping to open the flow of the energy systems in the body.

It challenges old belief systems and helps to dissolve them, in order to move into the new and unknown without fear.

Azurite initiates purification, renewal and transformational processes, and is good to use with other transcendental stones related to the Third Eye. Emotionally, azurite clears worry, grief, sadness and stress, transmuting fears and phobias.

Perhaps most significantly, azurite can open the gates of cosmic Truth and reveal the essential purpose of your life to you. It is a stone for highly evolved souls, and many find it an aid to their psychic development but will also discover that its effects are short-lived. It may therefore be best suited to receiving fleeting insights.

★ BERYL ★

Main Spiritual & Metaphysical Qualities ★ Encourages you to move along your rightful soul path; clarifies thoughts; releases deeply ingrained discordant belief systems; increases self-esteem; transformative.

Astrological Affinities ★ Depending on colour and variety, different varieties of beryl resonate with all zodiac signs; Water Element

Vibration ★ Earthy & High

Beryl, whose name is derived from the Greek, means 'shiny'. It is generally a transparent green stone, as well as being the name of a family of stones, which includes emerald and aquamarine. Other less known crystals in the same family are: bixbite, heliodor, morganite and goshenite. Members of this family have been used for healing, charms and jewellery for at least 4,000 years, although bixbite and morganite have only been identified more recently. Beryls were often made into amulets and talismans, carved with images of animals or plants to confer particular powers, and due to its luminous sea-green colouring it is sacred to all the oceanic deities.

Its gentle, natural energies make it a useful stone to work with in most areas of life, and it can aid divination, lucid dreaming, and strengthening of one's will. Stimulating the Third Eye Chakra, in magical workings beryl spheres have been used for scrying for over 2,000 years, and beryl and aquamarine are considered particularly good stones for helping to develop psychic and magical skills and abilities. Beryl was believed to encourage intelligence and manual and mental dexterity, and was used in crystallomancy to promote meditation, clairvoyance and concentration.

SOME CRYSTALS OF THE BERYL FAMILY:

Aquamarine ★ A sea-blue to sea-green stone, this semi-precious stone's name is derived from the Latin 'aqua marina', meaning 'sea water'. Aquamarine has been believed to bring good luck to lovers since the time of the Ancient Greeks and Romans. It works on the Sacral and Throat chakras and helps open you up to love.
Bixbite ★ A red to violet-coloured variety of beryl which can be used in love magic to call your 'twin soul'. It is also good for overcoming grief, loss, betrayal, emotional heartbreak, and to open the Heart chakra energy centre up to future love.
Emerald ★ A grass-green precious stone, whose name is derived from the Greek 'smaragdos', meaning 'green', emerald is mainly blue-green in colour but can also be green-yellow and even yellow. Virtues ascribed to this stone are that of hope, fertility and eternal youth. The Ancients believed that it would bestow immortality upon those who wore it. It has long been reputed to attract and retain true and committed love.
Goshenite ★ This colourless variety has been used to imitate gems, using a coloured foil backing, for around 2,000 years.
Heliodor ★ Otheriwse known as 'yellow beryl', this is a yellow to gold crystal, whose name is derived from the Greek meaning 'gift of the Sun'. This stone has a reputation for helping motivate the wearer and for enhancing quickness of the mind, due to the fact it is a Solar stone and the Sun is associated with success, drive, ambition, energy and power.
Morganite ★ A pink stone named after John Pierpont Morgan, an American banker who was interested in mineralogy and magic.

★ BLOODSTONE (HELIOTROPE) ★

The Fortifying Stone

Main Spiritual & Metaphysical Qualities ★ Instils courage & wisdom; protects the soul on many levels; enhances creativity, selflessness &

idealism; lends luck to competitive sports; strengthens will; heightens intuition; alleviates apathy, debility, low motivation, depression & disillusionment; stimulates dreaming; aids in decision-making; helps during times of transformation & change; enhances mental & emotional equilibrium; purifying, cleansing & healing on all levels.

Astrological Affinities ★ Aries, Libra, Sagittarius, Capricorn, Pisces, Mars, Venus, Fire Element

Magical Tips ★ Bloodstone raises your vibration and the courage of your convictions. Combined, these could help in manifesting your heart's deepest desires. Bloodstone has also been known to miraculously heal people. Because it has the magical ability to allow you to absorb the life force from it and heal yourself through this absorption, bloodstone has been used with great success on leukaemia patients, some of whom reported that their conditions significantly improved and even healed under its influence. It is known as an overall powerful healer and blood-cleanser, and apparently, as a true miracle-worker.

Vibration ★ Earthy

Also known as heliotrope, from the Greek words 'helios' meaning 'Sun', and 'trepein', meaning 'to turn towards', this alternate name stems from the belief in Ancient Greece and China that heliotrope could detect Solar eclipses, indicating the presence of the Moon as it

approached the Sun. Holding mightier than Mars energy but still relating to that planet, the bloodstone, with its traces of Plutonian influence, can give off an intense energy, and weigh heavily on the mind - for that reason, in healing it should always be used in combination with the more calming energies of blue or rose quartz, which will alleviate its oppressive effects.

According to myths, bloodstone has the power to detect changes in the heavens and therefore, is able to shroud things from view. The use of bloodstone stems from Ancient Babylon and Egypt, but the tale of its legendary origins are arguably more astounding than its powers. The blood of Christ, as he hung on the cross, was said to have splashed onto a piece of jasper below, tinging it with red and turning it into bloodstone. From this auspicious origin, this gemstone has been credited with the power to heal all manner of ailments, such as tumours, poor circulation, haemorrhaging, bloodshot eyes, snake bites, haemorrhoids, and even to protect the wearer from poison. The Egyptians believed that bloodstone could protect against deception, and worn as a protective amulet, it could help you see through lies.

Bloodstone is a dark green gemstone variety of chalcedony, a green jasper with red flecks. It is symbolic of courage, and it is also thought to bring its owner good fortune. Bloodstone has a variety of other magical abilities, including the power to stop blood from coming out of the body, increasing blood flow within the body, and enabling one to see the truth and win legal battles.

As a stone of intense 'life colours', it reminds us of our eternal connection to all living things. This stone can inspire bravery and, being aligned with Solar and Martian forces and sacred powers of healing, bloodstone is a useful crystal to work with to energise, protect, embolden, and empower. It is also said to fuel ambition and help one overcome inertia to improve one's work life in particular. It is believed to break down deep-rooted diseases and counteract overindulgence, obsession, violence and aggression, but in its lighter aspects, the bloodstone encourages a sunny disposition as it sweeps 'debris' from the chakras.

Other magical properties ascribed to this stone include realigning one with one's spiritual purpose, calming scattered thoughts, assisting in regeneration of the physical body, enhancing creativity, helping to make decisions, as well as imparting strength during periods of difficulty or loss of hope.

As it is connected with the Base or Root Chakra, as well as the Heart chakra (it is an excellent aid for grounding heart energy), it can give your lust and sex drive a boost, and increase your libido, clearing any blockages which may be restricting sexual expression, performance or desire.

Overall, bloodstone has beneficial effects on the heart, blood and circulatory system. Used as a healing stone for over 5,000 years, it maintains the energetic purity of the blood, which in ancient times was regarded as the Life Force.

Bloodstone is such a healing stone that it will promote healing on all levels when worn and help in overall attunement within one's own being. As its name suggests, bloodstone is an excellent blood cleanser, detoxifier, and all-round powerful healer.

★ CALCITE ★

Main Spiritual & Metaphysical Qualities ★ Cleanses & amplifies energy; empowers; motivates; stabilises.

Astrological Affinities ★ Depending on colour & variety, all zodiac signs; Aries, Leo, Fire Element

Magical Tips ★ Calcite is an excellent source by which we may tap into the element of calcium and all the healing properties it contains. Golden calcite carries the frequency of the yellow ray, meaning it is vibrating at the same speed as the colour yellow. This is the colour that activates the Solar Plexus chakra and because of that it is a stone that enables you to stand tall in your power, be courageous, and hold your ground. It contains a much more peaceful energy than citrine and is one of the most important stones of the Age of Aquarius. A nurturing, feel-good stone, honey calcite is the ultimate abundance-bringing crystal. Honey calcite is an effective manifestation stone, especially if you can find a piece of honeycomb to accompany it. Surround the honeycomb with golden-coloured crystals, flowers, fruit and jewellery, and regularly light beeswax candles to attract prosperity, abundance and fertility.

Calcite, a translucent, waxy, often banded gemstone, comes in over 700 varieties and a vast array of colours, such as green, yellow, blue, orange, brown, pink, grey, red and clear. The name calcite comes from the Latin calx (lime) and refers to its principal component, calcium. It is found in great abundance in the Earth's crust, in some 40 per cent of the surface rocks, and is part of the composition of many other minerals, from limestone to marble to alabaster.

In crystal therapy calcite is a powerful amplifier and cleanser of energy. It has been used for thousands of years for healing purposes, and each colour corresponds with unique therapeutic properties and different chakras within the body. However, most calcites regardless of colour, share some similar characteristics.

Calcite comes in many colours and varieties, and all of these have similar healing properties, depending on which one you are attracted to. Overall it is a soothing, protective stone that is excellent to calm the nerves. Simply having this stone in the room cleans negative energies from the environment and enhances your own power, and within the body it removes stagnant energy.

Calcite facilitates the increase of vitality on all levels; it combats laziness, encourages motivation, and has an overall positive, uplifting effect. Calcite is an active crystal, speeding up development and growth, and is also a spiritual stone linked to the higher consciousness. Indeed, it accelerates spiritual development and helps create emotional intelligence by connecting the emotions to the intellect. Calcite facilitates the opening up of psychic abilities, channelling, and astral connection.

Mentally, it calms the mind, instils discernment and analysis, boosts memory and stimulates insights, making it a useful stone for study. Emotionally, calcite alleviates emotional stress and restores serenity. A stabilising stone, it enhances group cooperation by transmuting negative energies and calling in higher forces to facilitate harmony between people.

Yellow calcite is believed to strengthen your ability to concentrate and helps to revitalise you. Known for bringing courage, golden calcite helps its user manifest ideas in the physical realm. It assists with the upward and downward flow of energy. It is known to purify the atmosphere and generate positive energy and helps to combat sadness and fortify one's self esteem. Because it stimulates the higher mind, it is generally used when working with the higher chakras, where it is thought to function as a great aid to meditation.

As it is known to be uplifting, calcite is particularly potent when taken in the form of an elixir, or gem essence.

★ CARNELIAN ★

Main Spiritual & Metaphysical Qualities ★ Promotes physical, mental & emotional vitality; restores motivation; lifts depression; aids optimism & joy; gives clarity of thought; promotes generosity; relaxing; enhances clarity of ideas; alleviates confusion & dissatisfaction with one's direction; eases hate, envy & jealousy.

Astrological Affinities ★ Aries, Taurus, Cancer, Leo, Virgo, Scorpio, Capricorn, Pisces, Saturn, Pluto

Magical Tips ★ In ancient times, carnelian was said to prevent misfortune and attract good luck. In the words of Goethe, "it brings good luck to child and man (and) drives away all evil things." Carnelian is believed to attract to you whatever you desire and turn dreams into reality, and as such is often used in abundance rituals and talismans. Carnelian also encourages gratitude for the good fortune of others, perpetuating and reinforcing the flow of universal abundance. Carnelian pieces placed by the front door of a home or business invokes protection and invites abundance into the dwelling.

Vibration ★ Earthy

Also known as cornelian or sard, carnelian is a type of chalcedony, taking its name from the Latin word 'cornu', which means 'horn', and among the many legendary powers surrounding it, are its remarkable properties as a stone of protection and great spirituality. It varies in colour from pink, orange, and blood-red to brownish or yellow, the colour deepening in direct sunlight.

Linked to the Base and Sacral chakras, this is a stabilising high-energy stone, and is particularly associated with sexual energy and fertility, said to encourage the kundalini (sexual energy/life force) to be more active; in this way, it could even be considered an aphrodisiac. Carnelian has a strong influence over the female reproductive system. As an activating stone that can help you in realising ideas and making plans manifest, it is a good stone to use if you are trying to become pregnant (both partners should use this crystal while trying to conceive).

Carnelian aligns the physical and etheric bodies, enhances attunement with the inner self, facilitates concentration, opens the heart and is generally warm, social and joyous. It releases stress and damage that is adversely affecting the etheric body, helps ease the trauma of abuse, and restores and improves the energy flow within the physical body.

Throughout history, carnelian has been used to discern the denizens of the astral plane, and to summon help from this domain. In Buddhism, it represented qualities such as faith, wisdom and perseverance, and in modern times the German literary figure Goethe connected powers of luck, protection, comfort and hope with this stone. The Egyptian *Book of the Dead* is a collection of papyrus scrolls that record in hieroglyphic text the wisdom of ancient priests and the experiences of the soul in the afterlife. Carnelian is mentioned a number of times in this book as it was regarded by the Egyptians as a protective stone and was used in many amulets, particularly those placed on the mummies of the rich and powerful.

The carnelian endows its wearer with contentment and self-confidence, and banishes fear, sorrow and the effects of the evil eye. It is believed to have therapeutic and curative effects against depression, chasing away dark thoughts, nightmares and bad moods. Because it instils a sense of confidence, it can give you the courage to speak your mind, and to overcome shyness, timidity or social inhibitions; it can also help you to trust yourself and your perceptions.

Carnelian is also excellent for restoring vitality and motivation, and stimulating creativity and dramatic pursuits. Carnelian can cleanse and re-energise other stones, and along with cinnabar, jade, turquoise, citrine, topaz and sunstone, can create and attract abundance into your experience.

Overall, carnelian's signature is strong, stimulating and protective. It is used to repair the etheric body after shock, loss, trauma or betrayal and ameliorates grief, including that associated with bereavement. So if you suffer from existential fears, past physical abuse, rage, resentment, vitality-sapping illness, or any long-standing mental anguish, the negativity-banishing properties of this stone are an effective ongoing life-force supplement. Perhaps its lesser known magical quality is that in meditation it can induce a better understanding of the true meaning of life and thus provide a key to insight and wisdom.

★ CAT'S EYE ★

Main Spiritual & Metaphysical Qualities ★ Grounding; protective; dispels negative energies; enhances intuition.

Astrological Affinities ★ Leo, Virgo

Magical Tips ★ The cat's eye has always been greatly valued in India, where it is regarded as a bringer of wealth - and a talisman to guard against the loss of wealth. A striking stone of beauty and playful magic, cat's eye is said to attract happiness, serenity, good fortune and luck.

Vibration ★ High

The Greeks called this crystal 'Waving Light', but it is better known as cat's eye. This name applies because a single whitish line appears to move when the stone is held towards the light and rotated, resembling the contracted pupil of a cat's eye; this effect is known as chatoyancy.

True cat's eye stones are made of a hard mineral called chrysoberyl. This especially valued, translucent gemstone may have a golden-yellow, bamboo-green or bluish-brown body, but whatever the tint, a powerful silver-white beam of light moves across its half-round or cabachon-cut surface when stimulated by movement.

Known as the 'stone-gourmet's delight', this stone's main characteristic, a bright green ribbon of light, occurs through reflection of light from fine, parallelled fibres or hollow crystal tubes which the growing crystal encased when forming.

Cat's eye has many magical properties. It is a grounding stone but is also effective at stimulating the intuitive functions. It is protective and dispels negative energy from the aura. Cat's eye is generally regarded as the most beautiful of the 'ray' gems and authentic pieces are priced accordingly.

★ CELESTITE ★

Main Spiritual & Metaphysical Qualities ★ Instils a profound sense of peace; promotes harmonious co-existence with the entire cosmos; enhances angelic communication; comforting in times of melancholy, reminding one that there is light & warmth at the end of darkness & winter; imbues hope & mental clarity; enhances intuition & instinct; stimulates creativity by expanding ideas.

Astrological Affinities ★ Gemini, Aquarius

Magical Tips ★ Celestite is a high vibration stone which uplifts and assists in bringing Divine energy into your experience. Use this crystal to call upon your guardian angel. Celestite placed on the Third Eye can open up the channels for psychic communication and connect to the star beings of the Pleiades (the Seven Sisters star cluster). Celestite is also a manifestation stone.

Vibration ★ High

The name celestite comes from the Latin *caelestis*, which literally means 'celestial' or 'heavenly', and in its ethereal blue form it lives up to its name, being a powerful crystal for cosmic connection.

Celestite aligns with the Throat, Third Eye and Crown chakras, and helps you connect with your higher self by clearing out left-brain clutter. This calming and relaxing stone aids meditation, creative expression, clear speech and expression, and accelerates spiritual growth. It connects you with the celestial wisdom of the Universal mind, and newcomers to crystal magic will find that celestite is perfect for bringing one into gentle contact with other dimensions. It assists in contacting spirit guides and gives access to the Akashic Record *, and allows astral travelling by helping you adjust to higher states of awareness.

A beautiful stone that forms baby blue crystals which emit calming rays, celestite assists in the healing of grief and facilitates the soothing and mending of a broken heart.

* The 'Akashic Record' is a cosmic record that exists beyond time and space, containing information on all that has occurred and all that will occur.

★ CHAROITE ★

Astrological Affinities ★ Sagittarius, Jupiter

Magical Tips ★ This stone, if you can find one, is a magical and mysterious dream-fulfiller with the ability to transform and manifest our deepest desires.

This is an expensive stone that is only found in one location in Russia, its rarity making it hard to come by. Its colours include pink, lilac, lavender, violet and vivid purple.

Having a particular affinity for the Third Eye, Crown and Heart chakras, charoite allows us to connect with the spiritual dimensions while still remaining grounded. One of the most highly evolved mineral healers of the purple ray, it accelerates spiritual growth by clearing emotional and mental blockages which are preventing you from changing your attitude. If you are resisting change, charoite will assist in breaking through the barriers.

Charoite is a stone of transformation, a gem with soul, that stimulates inner vision, spiritual wisdom and vibrational change. It enhances your ability to be loving and generous and encourages a path of service to humanity.

Charoite also alleviates deep fears, compulsions, obsessions and frustrations, and enhances drive, vigour, perspective, acceptance of others and unconditional love. Furthermore, it encourages deep, peaceful sleep and bestows powerful dreams, while at the same time warding off nightmares. It has the ability to transform fear into insight and eases emotional turmoil.

A stone of prophecy, charoite assists us in understanding our visions. Violet-coloured crystals such as charoite will help take you into a fantasy world, in which you can create or alter your reality. Stones of this hue can open the doors to other realms, release our fears, and remove obstacles from our paths.

Charoite is ultimately a cleanser and transmuter of negativity, clearing the aura and chakras, raising our self-esteem, and enabling us to express our unconditional love by opening up our hearts and spirits.

★ CHRYSOCOLLA ★

Main Spiritual & Metaphysical Qualities ★ Transmutes negative energy of all kinds; calms physical & emotional trauma; connects you to your Divine inner being; energises; powerfully vitalising to body & mind; encourages one to live one's truth & personal ideals; promotes compassion & forgiveness; instils a sense of self-trust.

Astrological Affinities ★ Taurus, Gemini, Leo, Virgo

Magical Tips ★ Chrysocolla is a calming and tranquillising stone and can be meditated with to instil a sense of peace or added to your bathwater to infuse your whole body, mind and spirit with calm.

Vibration ★ Earthy to High

Chrysocolla is one of the most beautiful and high energy stones there is. Its colour is a magnificent sky blue, coming mostly in striking shades of blue, green and turquoise. It is a tranquil, sustaining gem which helps meditation, dreaming and communication.

Chrysocolla resonates with the Throat and Heart chakras, encourages you to speak your Truth. It enhances insight which help clarify your spiritual purpose. It also connects and aligns us with Mother Earth, encouraging us to appreciate the balance of nature and to seek to attain this harmony within ourselves.

Chrysocolla balances, calms, cleanses and energises all the chakras and aligns them with the Divine. It helps one to invoke great inner strength amid change or chaos, helping one during stressful or long, enduring situations. Chrysocolla is especially beneficial for flailing relationships, assisting to re-build them. It dissolves guilt and helps to heal heartache, even increasing the capacity to love.

Chrysocolla also enhances personal power, creativity, self-awareness, motivation and inspires confidence and inner balance. Overall, this attractive stone is said to promote and activate love, wisdom, peace, friendship, success, luck, protection, and positivity.

★ CHRYSOPRASE ★

Astrological Affinities ★ Taurus, Gemini, Cancer, Libra, Scorpio, Sagittarius, Aquarius, Pisces, Pluto

Magical Tips ★ Carrying this stone for long periods of time can attune one to the devic * realm.

This crystal's magnificent rich tints, in cheerful shades of apple to lime green, are the main reason for its beauty and popularity. The most sought-after, nickel-tinted variety of Chrysoprase occurs in the town of Marlborough Creek in Queensland and comes in almost equally good quality from other parts of the world: California, Brazil, Russia, Poland and Tanzania.

Physically, chrysoprase has the potential to purge its wearer both physically and spiritually, from the lowest plane upwards. It has an outgoing influence, promoting inner clarity and discipline, and is adept in deflecting negative vibrations before they reach the higher senses. As jewellery or a touchstone, this mineral soothes nervous disorders, calms the brain before bursts of mental activity, steadies hysteria and convulsions, and eliminates anxiety. It also possesses a 'guard dog' character, protecting its wearer from overreactions and discordant factors until a balance has been reached. It supports and expands the Heart chakra, easing negative feelings and promoting joy. Its affinity with the Heart chakra gives it the ability to open, activate and energise the heart, and also to mend a broken one and to heal relationships.

Chrysoprase is useful for overcoming compulsive thoughts and actions, stimulating acceptance of oneself and others, fluent speech, mental dexterity, alleviating mental and physical exhaustion, reducing claustrophobia and nightmares, and encouraging forgiveness and compassion.

Resonating with the Sacral chakra, it can also be used to treat the reproductive organs and fertility problems. Chrysoprase, when placed over the Heart, Throat or Third Eye chakras, soothes and balances the system, and enhances the flow of positive feelings. Additionally, it attracts new love and abundance, and helps to prepare the system for new phases in life.

Carry or wear this gem to attract new relationships into your life, or put a piece under your pillow to improve the quality of your sleep. Overall, it encourages restful slumber and aids general relaxation.

Curiously, chrysoprase seems to be loyal to only one owner. On changing hands, or if its owner passes on, it may show no response at all under its new 'influence'.

* The term 'devic' relates to the kingdom of the devas, or nature spirits, believed to inhabit or reign over natural objects such as trees, mountains or bodies of water. People with clairvoyance are sometimes able to see or communicate with these spirits, by gaining intuitive access to the devic kingdom, the energetic level at which these entities exist.

★ CITRINE ★

The Joy & Abundance Stone

Main Spiritual & Metaphysical Qualities ★ Attracts abundance, wealth, luck, happiness & love; instils prosperity-consciousness; helps overcome doubt, fear, guilt or self-pity; enhances joy & living from one's core; encourages gratitude for life's bounty & joys.

Astrological Affinities ★ Aries, Gemini, Leo, Virgo, Libra, Scorpio, Sagittarius, Pisces, Fire Element

Magical Tips ★ Working with citrine will help you instinctively 'put out there' what you most wish to attract. If you use it with smoky quartz over the Base, Sacral and Solar Plexus chakras, it will help to activate the manifestation flow into your experience. Place citrine in the Wealth and Prosperity corner of your home (back left corner as you enter through the front door). It gives you the energy to manifest your desires and to attract everything that you need. Transmuting energy and radiating positivity, and holding the energy of wealth, keep this stone in your cashbox or purse to attract prosperity. Keep in mind that points attract *and* release energy, so a geode is perfect for 'collecting' and storing it. Citrine is sometimes referred to as the 'Merchant's Stone' because of its ability to bring wealth and prosperity to its owner. Citrine's energy is similar to that of the Sun ~ energising, life-giving and restorative. It brings the power of golden light into the material dimension of real life.

Vibration ★ High

Citrine is known in crystal healing circles as the success, prosperity, abundance and happiness stone, and is an attractive, bright, golden-yellow gem that takes its name from the old French word 'citron', meaning 'lemon' or 'yellow'. The golden-yellow colour of citrine quartz is formed when high temperatures are applied to amethyst or smoky quartz. Natural citrine is said to contain solidified sunlight and never to absorb negativity, so never needs cleansing (although it still benefits from regular purification).

Citrine carries the power of the Sun and has a particular affinity with the Solar Plexus chakra. Its beneficial energies also work well with the Sacral and Heart chakras. It is associated with good fortune, luck, abundance, manifestation, and increases personal power and energy. Citrine is an exceedingly beneficial stone, a powerful cleanser and regenerator, is warming, energising and highly creative. This is a willpower stone, having Solar affinities, and is particularly helpful for helping to release old patterns of behaviours or thoughts that stand in the way of our achieving greatness.

Being so sunny in nature, citrine energises every level of life, promotes clarity and puts us in touch with celestial Fire and the powers of our brightest luminary and the core essence of our self - the Sun; in this way, it can help to raise self-esteem and self-confidence. Because it is a stone of positivity, it dispels destructive tendencies, improves motivation, encourages self-expression, activates individuality, and is excellent for dissolving blockages to creativity. Further, it is useful for overcoming depression, fears and phobias, and promotes the inner calm that enables wisdom to emerge.

Citrine awakens the higher mind, stimulates inspiration and frees the mind of limitations, helping to turn ideas into reality. It amplifies and regenerates energy and being the product of heat-treated amethyst or smoky quartz, it carries the forces of transmutation and inner alchemy. Its bright yellow colour is literally like a sunbeam shining into your life, helping you to gain insight or confidence when you need to manifest change. This stone helps you look forward optimistically to the future instead of hanging onto the past; it also promotes exploration and enjoyment of new experiences.

Citrine is an aura protector and has the ability to cleanse the chakras, especially the Solar Plexus and Sacral chakras. But it also activates the Crown chakra, opens the intuition and balances the subtle bodies, aligning them with the physical. It is a good stone to use if you wish to develop your psychic abilities, especially if you have problems trusting and acting on your instincts. Hold a piece of citrine in your hand when you are undertaking any psychic work, such as mediumship or scrying, and it will enhance your inspiration and reasoning capacities. On a more physical level, citrine is good to wear or use when you have been subjected to chemicals, chemotherapy, and other toxins.

Citrine is one of the stones of abundance. This dynamic stone teaches how to attract, manifest and keep wealth, prosperity and success. Citrine has the power to impart joy to all who behold it, and overall it promotes joy in life. It is a happy, generous stone that encourages wonder, enthusiasm and delight, filling any dark areas with cheer and light. Citrine's sunny nature means that it can enliven you and connect you powerfully with the light of your inner being.

★ CORAL ★

Astrological Affinities ★ Aries, Taurus, Capricorn, Pisces, Mars, Mercury, Venus, the Moon

Magical Tips ★ Red coral is considered the best colour for protective charms and is called 'Witch Stone' in Italy. It was thought to absorb emotional negativity and was used against the Evil Eye.

Coral is among the most ancient of gem materials and was first used for adornment in prehistoric times. The name comes from a Greek word that means 'nymph of the sea'. Long regarded as a powerful talisman that was able to stop bleeding, give protection from evil spirits and even ward off hurricanes, red coral is renowned for its strength and energy. The wearing of coral was reputed to cure or prevent many ailments, and as an amulet it banished nightmares, protected children and warded off demons of the darkness, so in this sense it could be used as a protective gem.

The coral used in jewellery is the hard skeleton formed by certain polyps of the corallium nobile family and occurs in red, blue, golden, black, white and pink. These polyps are minute living creatures that live in vast colonies. When they die, their skeletal remains - mostly calcium carbonate - build up to form massive coral reefs.

Coral, particularly red coral, encourages one to have more determination and courage. As an ocean dweller, coral's astrological correspondence is with the Moon, which befits its watery genesis. It also resonates closely with the Lunar-ruled sign of Cancer.

★ When sourcing your coral, bear in mind that coral reefs are among the world's most vital yet fragile ecosystems, and materials taken from them should only be purchased from a reputable, ethical and sustainable marine operator.

★ DIAMOND ★

King of the Crystals

Class ★ Carbon
Crystalline Form ★ Cubic
Mohs Scale Hardness ★ 10
Colours ★ Colourless with brilliant lustre
Clarity & Brilliance ★ Transparent, admanatine shine
Chakra ★ Crown, all

Main Spiritual & Metaphysical Qualities ★ Stimulates spirituality; confers inner peace & serenity; increases courage and physical strength; eases depression; increases fertility; expands consciousness; assists in soul evolution.

Astrological Affinities ★ Aries, Taurus, all zodiac signs, all planets

Magical Tips ★ If you receive a diamond that had a previous owner, it is a good idea to cleanse the stone with water and sunlight before wearing it, since diamonds can keep vibrations in them. To be efficacious as a talisman (magical charm), the diamond should be given freely, never sold, never lent, never coveted, and never taken by fraud or force. The six-cornered stone is thought to bring the best of good fortune and to renew one's strength. Overall, diamonds bring clarity to all that needs to be transmuted and transformed. Put your trust in it to do its work efficiently and effectively.

Vibration ★ High

Universally considered the greatest of stones, the diamond has been revered throughout the ages for its beauty and strength. The Ancient Greeks believed that diamonds were actually splinters of stars that had fallen to Earth, and it was thought by some they were the tears of the gods.

Diamond is pure crystallised carbon and is known as the supreme ruler of the mineral kingdom, due to its hardwearing qualities, sparkle, hardness, shine, and sheer brilliance.

Diamond is the purest substance in nature and one of the hardest (10 out of 10 on the Mohs scale). It's little wonder they are so expensive: when found, the diamond is covered with a thick crust, so hard that there is no substance known that will remove it but that of itself. And it is only by grinding and polishing with diamond dust and minute diamonds that it is shaped and a jewel's wonderful brilliancy emerges and develops. In other words, the only thing that can cut a diamond is another diamond. Mined for over 4,000 years, ancient civilisations discovered that this amazing gem could cut any other stone.

The word 'diamond' has its origin in the Greek word 'adamas', which means unconquerable. The diamond is known universally as a token of love; quite simply, it is the ultimate symbol of purity. This luminously brilliant gem, through its renowned purity and durability, offers incomparable proof of total perfection expressed in a single element.

Diamond's pure white light can help to bring your life into a cohesive whole, the first step in using your power to optimum effect. It bonds relationships, is said to enhance a husband's love of his wife, brings enchantment and clarity into a partnership, and is seen as a sign of commitment and faithfulness.

Psychologically, this precious gem imparts a sense of fearlessness, fortitude and invincibility, for diamonds are unbreakable in every sense of the word.

Diamond is also an amplifier of any energy with which it comes into contact, therefore should only be used for positive spells and magic and is one of the few stones that never needs recharging or cleansing; in fact, it increases the energy of whatever it comes into contact with and is very effective when used with other crystals for healing as it enhances and draws out their power.

Like the clear quartz, the diamond is a master healer which accelerates the spiritual development of its wearer. As an amplifier of energy, the merciless light of diamond will highlight anything that is negative and requires transformation.

Diamond has been a symbol for wealth for thousands of years and is one of the stones of manifestation, with the ability to attract abundance; the larger the diamond, the more abundance will be drawn to the requester.

Diamond helps to clear emotional and mental pain, alleviates fear and brings about new beginnings. It also provides a link between the intellect and the higher mind, aiding clarity and enlightenment of mind. On a spiritual level, it allows one's soul light to shine out, cleansing the aura of anything shrouding the inner light, and reminds you of your soul's aspirations; it is the ultimate activator of the Crown chakra, linking one to the 'Divine Light' and highest planes of being.

Indeed, clear crystals such as diamond will interact with your energy field by raising your vibration through clearing away any cloudiness or blockages within your subtle bodies. A highly creative stone, stimulating imagination and inventiveness, and aiding spiritual evolution, diamond has certainly earned its reputation as 'King of the Crystals'.

★ DIOPTASE ★

Main Spiritual & Metaphysical Qualities ★ Facilitates spiritual attunement; promotes emotional stability; dissolves emotional pain & grief; activates past life memories; stimulates intuition.

Astrological Affinities ★ Virgo, Scorpio, Sagittarius

Dioptase often comes in a glittering cluster of hypnotic green crystals arguably more vibrant than any emerald. In fact, this rare and expensive stone rivals the emerald in both the beauty of its colouring and its holistic powers. One of the most highly spiritual stones, dioptase brings a heightened state of awareness, emotional stability, and the gift of raised consciousness to its wearer.

Not suitable for cutting due to its brittle nature, this crystal is a powerful healer for the heart and opens the higher Heart chakra. Its beautiful deep-green colouring raises the functioning of all the chakras and has a dramatic effect on the human energy field, facilitating great spiritual attunement.

Dioptase appears in brilliant small crystals which sit on a host rock, usually on a matrix, and if found in pendant form (many a magnificent rich-green pendant has been fashioned around a nest of natural dioptase crystals), this jewel should be worn mid-chest where it can affect its most powerful benefits.

Dioptase is a strong mental cleanser and detoxifier, acting as a bridge to emotional healing. It assists in dissolving and easing the pain associated with abandonment, heartache, grief, betrayal and sorrow. As such, dioptase teaches that ultimately challenge and difficulty in a relationship is a reflection of an inner separation from the *Self*. It can repair any such broken links and draw in love at all levels, filling in emotional 'black holes', clearing away old perceptions and notions of how love should be, and bringing in a new vibration. It can be programmed for use with affirmations that enhance self-esteem and self-worth.

Dioptase supports a more positive attitude to life and overcomes any sense of lack. It can also enable the fulfilling of one's innate potential and can indicate direction when you are unsure of what to do next. Dioptase encourages living in the present moment, and paradoxically also activates past-life memories. Aligning both the physical and etheric bodies, it is also excellent for cellular regeneration and healing.

Spiritually, dioptase can raise awareness of one's inner riches by enhancing spiritual and psychic attunement and receptivity, sharpening extrasensory perception (ESP) faculties, and drawing in guidance from higher planes when placed upon the Third Eye.

★ EMERALD ★

The Emerald is one of the precious stones with the greatest gift of curative power because it is effective against all human frailties and disabilities; in fact, it is the Sun which creates it and its entire substance is made from the vitality of the air.

Extract from *The Works of St Hildegarde of Bingen*

Main Spiritual & Metaphysical Qualities ★ Attracts love; enhances optimism & hope; strengthens the ability to love & open up to others; calms the emotions; generates spiritual peace; promotes understanding & empathy; enhances meditation; balances emotions; brings equilibrium.

Astrological Affinities ★ Aries, Taurus, Gemini, Cancer, Leo, Virgo, Scorpio, Pisces, Venus, Mercury, the Moon, Jupiter

Magical Tips ★ Emeralds were a prime source of wealth in Ancient Greece and Egypt, and this legacy endures today. Emerald is believed to attract good fortune. Wear emerald to attract and retain successful love. It enhances relationships and love on all levels.

Vibration ★ Earthy

Emerald is a vivid grass-green precious stone belonging to the beryl family, whose name is derived from the Greek *beryllos*, meaning a green stone. Emerald is mainly blue-green in colour but can also be green-yellow and even yellow.

Virtues ascribed to this stone are that of hope, purity, prosperity, love, dreams, kindness, healing, fertility and eternal youth; the ancients believed that it would bestow immortality and good fortune upon those who wore it. With its dazzling green brilliance, emerald has long been prized for its magical properties and as such has a long history of myth and folklore. Most important of all was emerald's reputation as a link with the Divine forces. It is said to enhance psychic abilities and clairvoyance. Emerald is a powerful stone, associated with natural elements such as the Moon, water and rain. It is also linked with alchemists and with the Greek god Hermes, and its legendary healing powers are said to be closely linked to the occult. The ancients believed that Hermes inscribed the laws of 'magic', the thirteen precepts, upon the famed Emerald Tablets. Indeed, emeralds were dedicated to Mercury, the winged messenger and Hermes' Roman counterpart, by early astrologers.

Connected with the Heart chakra, emerald opens and activates this vital organ to heal all problems associated with the heart, whether they be physical or emotional. It is known as 'the stone of successful love' with which unconditional love can be pledged to a partner. Possessing a very loving vibration, emerald carried in the left pocket is said to attract this vibe to you. To increase the loving vibration of your interaction with others, i.e. what you send out, carry this stone in your right pocket.

By promoting harmony and wholeness to every aspect of one's life, emerald dispels negativity and draws beauty, wisdom and healing to it. Emerald ensures emotional, physical and mental equilibrium and imparts strength of character to overcome setbacks and misfortunes. As a stone of regeneration and recovery, it can inspire a deep inner knowing, broaden vision, and enhance one's wisdom and integrity. Indeed, in ancient times, emerald was seen as a stone which could deliver knowledge of mysteries, bringing particular wisdom and inspiration, and served both as a remedy and a miracle stone.

This rich, deep green stone encourages us to follow the laws of nature and, by imbuing us with a sense of beauty and openness, enhances our ability to appreciate the wonders of life. Emerald encourages gratitude, helping you to recognise abundance and beauty in all their forms.

Perfect, sellable emerald stones are rare; most are cloudy, unremarkable or otherwise flawed - but can still be effectively used for healing purposes - after all, their appearance doesn't affect their composition.

Life-affirming, attractive and inspirational, this brilliant green-hued variety of beryl instils a sense of vitality, love and energy, and is an overall uplifting and healing tonic for the mind, body and spirit.

★ FLOURITE ★

Main Spiritual & Metaphysical Qualities ★ Brings inner peace & strength; increases intuition & capacity for depth of thought; calms & controls strong & negative emotions such as fear & rage; promotes harmony between reason & sentiment; helps us to find the path leading to truth & wisdom; general stabilising effect; cleanses the aura.

Astrological Affinities ★ Pisces

Magical Tips ★ Fluorite derives its name from the Latin word 'fluere' meaning 'to flow' and has a very unusual quality - it gives off light in darkness when exposed to a source of heat; under ultra-violet lighting, fluorite emits a beautiful glow - hence the term 'fluorescence'.

Vibration ★ Earthy

Fluorite, also known as fluorspar, usually has a basic white body, but can be angelically coloured in the softest shades of pink, magenta, black, green, white, purple, yellow and blue. It is often found in limestone caverns and as a natural cement in sandstone. Fluorite crystals usually grow in cubes.

Green and purple fluorite is a popular choice, and these two complementary shades are linked to the Heart (green) and the Crown (purple) chakras, so together can be said to symbolise Divine Love. Green is the colour of expansion, love, growth and new beginnings, while purple is the shade associated with spiritual ascension and awareness of higher levels of consciousness. Thus the two colours combined enable the wisdom of heightened awakenings to enter the physical body and reside in the heart.

Meditating with this crystal can encourage a gentle and flowing sense of peace through the whole system, an ideal state in which to experience spiritual expansion and one's unfolding into new levels of insight and consciousness. Furthermore, it has a harmonising effect on the body on account of its ability to balance the nervous system, as well as encouraging harmony and stability in relationships.

As a stone which endows the mind with discernment and clarity, fluorite increases our concentration and is a useful study aid, enabling us to absorb information rapidly. It can also be used on the Third Eye chakra to bring about greater clarity of vision and light the way to a clearer path ahead. Purple fluorite is a wonderful stone for meditation that not only helps the mind to focus, but opens up our intuitive faculties, reveals truths, allows us to see through any veils of illusion, and enhances psychic abilities.

Overall, fluorite acts to cleanse, purify, dispel and reorganise any aspects within the body or surroundings that are not in perfect order; it can overcome chaos and set about resetting and restructuring the physical, mental and emotional bodies, thus allowing higher spiritual energy to be quickly absorbed and integrated.

Fluorite eases physical and emotional stress, helps to balance the mind, body and spirit, and cleanses and replenishes the energy field surrounding the body. As it cleanses and stabilises the aura, it is also extremely effective against computer and electromagnetic stress.

★ GARNET ★

Main Spiritual & Metaphysical Qualities ★ Powerfully energising; regenerative; revitalising; purifying; balancing; protective; transmutes pain, dis-ease & discordant emotions into well-being; instils courage & stamina.

Astrological Affinities ★ Aries, Cancer, Leo, Virgo, Scorpio, Sagittarius, Capricorn, Aquarius, Mars, Fire Element

Magical Tips ★ Garnet is a powerful attractor of abundance, and grossular garnet or hexagonal green garnet are effective stones for creating a pentacle layout in magical workings. It is traditionally believed that wearing a square-cut garnet encourages success in business dealings. As it brings hope, carry it when you are feeling you will never achieve your goals; it gives you the power to succeed in seemingly hopeless situations. Garnet can also activate other crystals, amplifying their effect.

Vibration ★ Earthy to High

Garnet, whose name comes from the word 'grain', is a bright to dark red compound silicate. It is regarded as a symbol of sincerity, good faith, loyalty and honesty. This stone is one of vitality and dreams and increases the flow of the body's natural energy systems. Sometimes known as 'carbuncles' (when they are cut *en cabachon*, that is flat at the bottom or with a convex rounded top instead of facets), garnets occur in many different shades, the most well-known being deep, dark red.

Relating to the mysteries of sex and regeneration, garnet is a stimulant and effective connector to our deepest memories. It is a useful stone to have during challenges and lawsuits, where courage or fortitude may be required. During such times of change or upheaval, it can provide a sense of grounding, calm and balance. It also inspires service, cooperation, relaxation and 'going with the flow'.

Garnet has an affinity for the Base and Sacral chakras, where it breaks down blockages and stimulates our untapped creative energy. It will also revitalise and balance energy in these chakras, bringing serenity, acceptance or passion according to the need.

Being a stone of the Base chakra, which governs our security and survival needs, garnet keeps us grounded, making us feel safe and secure. Garnet can help lift melancholy and will help you find your inner strength and full potential by releasing your fear of failure. As such, it assists in boosting confidence, imparting courage, building strength of character, and enables us to find our inner fortitude and resources. Garnet helps to dissolve unhelpful behavioural patterns and past hurts to allow you to become more self-empowered and move on. Further, if you are feeling impotent or stuck in plans that have not yet manifested, this stone assists in moving out of the stagnancy and into potent action. It is also useful in easing situations in which you feel trapped and there seems no way out, or where life has become chaotic or broken, offering hope in apparently hopeless circumstances.

Garnet can help with any sexual difficulties, both mentally and physically, and is a stone of love and commitment which brings warmth, devotion, constancy, faithfulness, understanding, sincerity, trust and honesty to a relationship. Garnet's innovative vibration encourages you to be more creative and stimulates the right brain, creating 'light-bulb' flashes of inspiration and thought.

Carrying a powerful red ray, garnet draws prosperity into your experience, increases generosity and vitality, and offers support during challenges. It is interesting to note that skyscrapers built on New York's Manhattan Island have deep foundations driven into the island's bedrock, which contains a vast amount of garnet.

Overall, garnet is an energising and regenerative stone, especially for the two lowest bodily chakras, although it also works effectively on the Heart chakra.

★ GOLDSTONE ★

The Alchemy Crystal

Main Spiritual & Metaphysical Qualities ★ Attracts wealth; enhances inner magic.

Astrological Affinities ★ Gemini, Leo

Magical Tips ★ Goldstone is a manmade stone created from glass and copper through the process of alchemy, and this imbues it with a magical essence, helping you to perform financial alchemy that can transform your life. Created out of the fires of transmutation, this sparkling stone represents pure transformation and prosperity.

Thought to have been first made in Venice in the 17th century by the Miotti, an ancient glass-making family, goldstone may have even been made long before that by alchemists as they attempted to make gold. Whatever its true origins, goldstone is popular today for jewellery and the belief that it increases wealth.

Goldstone is a generator stone which is associated with drive, ambition, self-confidence, and a positive attitude which encourages you to take risks. Goldstone helps you to find your inner wealth and instils the patience that enables you to wait until the time is ripe for its revelation. When used in prosperity layouts, rituals, askings and spells, goldstone stimulates the process of 'like attracts like' and when worn as jewellery it holds an activating quality, retaining its transmutative powers and purity of intention over a long period of time.

Goldstone is said to clear and energise the chakras. It dissipates fearfulness, alleviates stress and increases vitality. Goldstone encourages independence and originality. Above all, it reminds you of your deep well of inner riches and encourages the concept of, "As within, so without".

★ HELIODOR ★

Astrological Affinities ★ Leo

Magical Tips ★ This lemon to rich-yellow transparent power crystal has the potential to be a medium of great spiritual illumination.

Golden-hued heliodor is a type of beryl which forms through extreme pressure and high temperatures. Heliodor, or golden beryl as it is also known, heals stress in the mental body by activating and integrating the Crown and Solar Plexus chakras. It opens gateways to our understanding of archetypal realms, and by giving you this greater insight into the role you are playing in your life drama, it allows you to step out of the illusion to view your true situation more clearly, which in turn promotes greater psychological and emotional stability. It consoles, rejuvenates and achieves its powerful effects through its ability to reconcile the conscious and the unconscious mind.

Although heliodor works essentially through the Solar Plexus, it actually resonates most strongly with the circulatory system and the heart, where it operates to energise the inner self and the intellect - and indeed, to link the two. Also, by expanding your Crown chakra to bring in higher guidance, it allows your Solar Plexus chakra to shine with more clarity and the essence of the Sun. The expanded self-awareness that results will facilitate the broadening of perspective where false judgments and delusions about yourself and others can be dissolved and released.

Often showing radioactivity and generally thought to be tinted by iron, both of which are emitted by and associated with the Sun, heliodor resembles a solid chunk of golden light, and in healing radiates a corresponding warmth.

★ HEMATITE ★

Main Spiritual & Metaphysical Qualities ★ Aids concentration; increases energy; imbues strength & courage; promotes inner peace & calm; aids reason & intellect; assists memory; grounding; balancing; balances yin & yang; enhances self-esteem; strengthens personal magnetism & power.

Astrological Affinities ★ Aries, Gemini, Scorpio, Capricorn, Aquarius

Magical Tips ★ Possessing the ability to carry magnetism, hematite can be used for both drawing and release. Many of hematite's curative powers are related to its magnetic properties, and the mineral is credited with the ability to attract love and friendship, fulfil desires, increase intelligence and confer powers of persuasion. Allowing for mental clarity, if you hold a piece of this stone tightly in your hand and ask a question, you will find that the stone will help the answer come to you.

Vibration ★ Earthy

Deriving its name from the Greek 'haema' referring to the colour of rust and meaning 'blood', hematite is one of the main sources of iron ore and has many healing uses. Usually occurring as black and dark grey crystals, when polished it can have the appearance of a perfect spherical mirror. Ranging from metallic to brilliant, it is usually lead grey.

Hematite is a heavy metallic stone that absorbs negativity and is capable of drawing illness away from the body. Also known as the worry stone, hematite is calming to the emotions and is considered an excellent gem for maintaining a balance between body, mind and spirit.

Hematite is an effective amulet for strength and courage if you are involved in a battle of wills or words, such as in a courtroom situation. Likewise, keep a piece of hematite with you to help you succeed in legal battles, or at least instil a sense of fortitude.

Strengthening the Base chakra, this is a wonderfully effective gentle grounding stone, useful for when one is feeling scattered or chaotic. It is also flexible and seems to know the right amount of grounding you are needing without weighing you down and will give you that level of stability needed accordingly. Being a grounding stone, if you have a sense that your life is fragmented and needing a sense of security and coherence, obtain a piece of hematite, consecrate it with the four elements and carry or wear it as a charm; this is believed to restore harmony in your life.

Being an iron-based crystal, it is not surprising that hematite was a popular stone with warriors in times past. It was believed that rubbing the body with hematite would confer strength, bravery and invincibility on a warrior, ensuring victory. Hematite is also reputed to impart courage if you are feeling you are not able to say what you mean or to speak out against something you know to be wrong - by rubbing it on your Throat chakra, it can inspire you with the strength of the warrior, encourage the power of your convictions to come forth, and bestow a fiercer spirit of expression and determination.

Hematite carries the deep energy of the Earth and overall it is known to possess powerful energising properties. The link between iron and the Earth's magnetic field could be responsible for the seemingly endless supply of energy this gemstone imparts. Combined with quartz it becomes red jasper, a stone which is also rich in healing and protective attributes.

★ JADE ★

Main Spiritual & Metaphysical Qualities ★ Boosts confidence; aids meditation; heals emotional trauma; induces insightful dreams; soothes; helps to improve & strengthen overall health; increases perception & self-understanding; instils the five virtues of wisdom, modesty, justice, courage & purity; blesses one with the five happinesses of love of virtue, wealth, old age, natural death & health; restores the soul's purity; symbolises good fortune.

Astrological Affinities ★ Taurus, Gemini, Virgo, Libra, Aquarius, Pisces, Venus, Earth Element

Magical Tips ★ Jade has a long history of being used to attract wealth and prosperity due to its associations with royalty. The ancients considered jade a sacred stone and it was traditionally worn as a stone of good fortune. Placing a piece of jade in your work space is believed to attract wealth and enhance calm and harmony in the work environment. The Chinese call jadeite 'Yu Shih' meaning Yu stone, believing it to contain all five cardinal virtues needed for a happy existence: modesty, courage, charity, justice and wisdom. Maori greenstone jade is a master healer and powerful manifestor, and the Chinese attest that jade will bring harmony and health to your home when used ornamentally. Confucius said jade had several virtues, including benevolence, wisdom, fidelity, and sincerity.

Vibration ★ Earthy to High

Jade is a stone that is greatly valued by the Chinese, who believe that it brings clarity, modesty, courage, justice and wisdom.

Two crystals are commonly known as jade by the gem trade: jadeite and nephrite. Although nephrite and jadeite are two distinct minerals with differing holistic values, they do share many similarities. Jadeite was recognised as a separate mineral in 1863 by a French chemist, who analysed two separate specimens from China and found them to be different minerals. Since nephrite was firmly established, he called the second specimen jadeite. Jadeite's colours range through green, white, pink, black, yellow and mauve, with green being probably the most well-known. The most sought-after colouring is an intense apple green, an eye-catching, extremely rare and highly attractive gem also known as Imperial Jade.

Jade brings peace through serenity and cleanses the energy centres. This creamy, sacred stone is believed to bring good fortune, prosperity and longevity to its owner. It is also said to be a symbol of Divine revelation.

Green jade strengthens the Heart chakra and can be used to harmonise dysfunctional relationships. It calms the nervous system and channels passion in constructive ways. Providing a link between the spiritual and the mundane, jade stimulates practicality and wisdom. It increases love and nurturing and symbolises harmony, purity, protection, good luck and friendship.

Jade is a serenity stone and balances the nervous system, dispelling moods swings and calming anger and irritability. It is also said to stabilise the temperament and instil a sense of tranquillity. It is an excellent tonic for healing conditions associated with stress and feelings of overwhelming obligation. A wonderful ally in healing others, jade is a good stone for those who are beginner healers or who wish to give their healing skills an added boost.

On a spiritual level jade has an affinity for the Heart chakra and it harmonises relationships, encourages compassion and the establishment of strong bonds.

Jade brings composure when it is worn, carried or used, and instils wisdom. Chinese business people have extensively used jade to attract new business and promote worthy causes and ventures. Used with other stones or on its own, it is traditionally believed to generate abundance and attract good fortune in all areas of life.

Jade is also a useful 'dream' stone; placed under your pillow, it encourages insightful dreams and will help you to not only remember your dreams, but also to interpret them. As well as being good for promoting the dream-state, this is a good stone for using under your pillow to encourage deep and restful sleep. In addition, as a stone of wisdom, it assists you to reach decisions about meaningful things.

Spiritually, jade encourages you to become who you really are. Awakening hidden knowledge within yourself, it assists in recognising yourself as a spiritual being on a human journey. A profoundly spiritual stone, jade encourages you to recognise that you have access to much wider powers and dimensions than can be physically seen, and as such motivates you to become all that you can be. It can also assist your understanding of any blocks which may be hindering the manifestation or progress of your goals. Jade has the wonderful attribute of dispelling all negativity.

A gentle and effective healer, nephrite jade is grounding, centring and brings strength. It can be used when undergoing surgery as it will help calm the nerves and is peace-promoting. As well, it transmutes anger into acceptance and assists in forgiving those who have hurt you. Nephrite provides a barrier of protection for sensitive people against negative vibrations and energies. It assists in decision-making concerning spiritual and emotional matters and helps to release and transform fear into more positive emotions. Jade is balancing and harmonising for the Sacral, Root and Heart chakras.

★ JADE ~ LAVENDER JADEITE ★

Astrological Affinities ★ Sagittarius, Pisces, Jupiter

Magical Tips ★ When struck with a resonant instrument, jadeite gives a musical note, which probably gave rise to the ancient belief that it was a 'charm of harmonious omen'.

Lavender jadeite is a pale pinkish purple stone which emanates pure energy of the highest etheric spectrum. It provides spiritual nourishment, is excellent for meditation, and helps one to cultivate and embrace an attitude of serene acceptance.

In addition to the generic attributes of jade, lavender jadeite (or jade) alleviates emotional hurt and trauma, releases cynicism and bestows a sense of inner peace. Its higher guidance and connection with the cosmic and etheric planes expands spiritual-emotional awareness and encourages empathy.

Lavender jade teaches subtlety and restraint in emotional matters, gently holding back the excessive expression of feelings, and helps to set clear boundaries.

Lavender jadeite, like its better known 'sister' green jade, has an affinity for the Heart chakra, and both open up the heart on an emotional, as well as physical level. Being of the violet-purple ray, it is also a powerful tonic for the Third Eye chakra, opening one up to Divine channels and assistance.

Emotionally lavender jade encourages compassion and the establishment of strong bonds. Overall it is balancing to the nervous system, dispelling mood swings, and calming anger and irritability. A stone of spiritual wisdom, lavender jade helps us to reach wise decisions too. It is a potent symbol of purity, steadfastness and all things enduring.

★ JASPER ★

Main Spiritual & Metaphysical Qualities ★ Instils courage; encourages self-honesty; nurturing; enhances wisdom; facilitates karmic healing; stabilises & energises; cleanses, boosts & realigns energy.

Astrological Affinities ★ Aries, Leo, Virgo, Scorpio, Mercury

Magical Tips ★ Green jasper has traditionally been associated with luck - a jasper arrowhead was said to bring the bearer good fortune, and a green jasper talisman with the symbol of Aquarius engraved on it was carried by traders to enhance their sales.

Vibration ★ Earthy

Jasper is a chalcedony which comes in a variety of colours - brown, orange, red, yellow and green being the most common. The green colour when flecked with red, is known as bloodstone. Each colour corresponds with a different chakra, and all can be used for aligning the chakras, promoting wellbeing and overall healing purposes.

The Ancients believed in jasper's power to lighten the spirit, bring comfort, to relax and even to make childbirth easier. Jasper has been used in charms around the world for many centuries; from Ancient Greece and Egypt to the Americas, jasper was considered a sacred and protective stone which was worn or carried to protect the bearer from misfortune, such as from a range of maladies including poisoning, insanity, 'possession' and evil spirits.

Yellow jasper balances the Solar Plexus chakra, calms the nerves and is an overall protective stone, protecting during both spiritual and physical travel 'journeys'. Both grounding and stabilising, this stone has a special ability to take control of uncontrolled or unfocused energy. Having a grounding energy makes this stone useful for connecting with the Earth and focusing one's thoughts on solidity and form. Also protective, wearing or carrying jasper can make you less susceptible to negative influences, such as being the subject of slander or gossip.

Jasper has had a long reputation as a healing stone and also as a rain-bringer. Emotionally, it absorbs negativity and aligns the chakras and the aura. It imparts determination and encourages assertiveness and honesty with oneself. It also stimulates the imagination and transforms ideas into action. It can help fight anxiety and inspire confidence. Overall, jasper is known as the 'supreme nurturer', being supportive and sustaining during times of stress, and bringing tranquillity and wholeness to one's spirit in times of trouble.

★ JASPER ~ RED ★

Main Spiritual & Metaphysical Qualities ★ Helps to overcome depression; strengthens sexual desire; increases one's capacity for enjoyment; grounding; balancing; instils passion & courage.

Astrological Affinities ★ Aries, Scorpio, Mars, Earth Element

Magical Tips ★ Ancient Greeks wore it above the heart as a talisman to awaken love. A particularly good stone to use for feng shui symbols of good fortune, the red colour indicates the presence of yang energy. It also reveals the presence of hematite, which the ancient Chinese regarded as the most valuable of Earth stones. Because of its physically porous character, red jasper easily absorbs energy, making it an optimal regenerator of vibrations.

Red jasper is one of the many varieties of chalcedony. A slightly brownish, red colour, red jasper has been a sacred stone over many millennia. It resonates most with the Sacral chakra, which is related to sexual function, and whose activation allows us, on a spiritual level, to be in more vivid contact with everything that is pleasant and sensual in our experience.

Placing two pieces of red jasper on one's bedside table is believed to attract and increase sexual passions in one's experience. It is a powerful love attractor.

Red jasper has balancing and grounding properties and is also attuned to the Base Chakra, bestowing courage, passion, and the willpower to achieve one's goals. Excellent for stimulating the circulation and increasing energy, red jasper is also a nurturing stone that is helpful in times of recovery. It cleanses and stabilises the aura and offers a shield of protection through strengthening your boundaries. As a Base chakra balancer, red jasper helps one to overcome depressive moods, strengthens sexual desire, instils a strong sense of security and grounding, increases your capacity for enjoyment, and infuses you with fortitude and bravery.

Red jasper is said to affect the psychic, as well as the physical and emotional planes of existence and as a result, is often recommended by gem therapists for fighting depression, melancholy and apathy. Its power over the field of emotions and feelings is also important, as it is considered particularly effective for timid or insecure people, helping them to fight fear and anxieties around expressing amorous love.

Overall, red jasper awakens intense feelings and passions, and infuses you with courage, desire, and emotional strength.

★ JASPER ~ IRON TIGER EYE / TIGER IRON ★

Main Spiritual & Metaphysical Qualities ★ Grounding; heightens creativity; promotes self-confidence; stimulates energy; enhances clarity of mind, strength, courage, willpower, alertness & initiative; alleviates fears; lifts apathy; accelerates healing.

Astrological Affinities ★ Scorpio, Earth Element

Iron tiger eye jasper or tiger iron, is a variety of tiger's eye, and is a brilliant crystal which consists of three constituents: tiger eye, jasper and hematite, which all share the same quality of grounding - the ability to pull together scattered emotional and mental energy. Tiger eye jasper is an important healing stone, combining the properties of its three minerals, and is a stable healing gem that rarely needs cleansing.

Tiger eye jasper is believed to promote self-confidence and self-assurance and to improve energy and stamina in people who undertake physical exertion in their day-to-day lives. It is also a creative stone, assisting in all kinds of artistic endeavours.

Tiger iron breathes new life into creative pursuits, helps one to focus on goals, aids multi-tasking, and encourages motivation. It is sometimes called 'the protective stone', and is used to combat apathy and exhaustion, to promote emotional stability, to reinforce self-esteem, and to help one face confronting or difficult situations.

Due to its colouration, from earthy browns to deep golden oranges, tiger iron's properties are closely linked to all Earth symbolism, such as grounding, protection, sustenance, growth, stability, development, equilibrium, and a sense of rootedness, strength, security, and power.

Overall, tiger iron's vibrations are said to help to renew energy and restore self-esteem and help one overcome feelings of deep sadness and grief, as it imparts a sense of emotional and mental fortitude.

★ JASPER ~ YELLOW ★

Main Spiritual & Metaphysical Qualities ★ Long associated with health, wealth & happiness; increases self-confidence; helps to overcome stress & states of depression & profound sadness; increases spiritual & emotional strength; encourages independence; protective during travel; imparts courage; assists bravery & achievement.

Astrological Affinities ★ Gemini, Leo, Virgo

Yellow jasper is a variety of chalcedony that sometimes has golden tones. In times past, yellow jasper was used in rituals to attract happiness and to banish misfortune and illness. It has always been associated with health, prosperity, wellbeing and wealth, largely due to its bright golden colour, which naturally links it with the Sun, and all the properties of our biggest, brightest Star.

Used in the home, yellow jasper is believed to create an energy field that purifies surroundings, clearing them of negative energy. In crystal therapy, specifically programmed pieces of yellow jasper are often indicated for use as an energiser. Due to its particular link with the Solar Plexus chakra, seen as the seat of powerful emotions and 'gut instincts', the use of this stone to overcome emotional issues, melancholy, fears and phobias, is believed to produce effective results.

Yellow jasper's ability to strengthen us spiritually makes it an invaluable addition to any crystal therapy work.

★ JET ★

Main Spiritual & Metaphysical Qualities ★ A positive, calming influence; balancing; emotionally cleansing; tranquillising; combats nightmares; invigorating; alleviates mood swings; protects overall health.

Astrological Affinities ★ Saturn, Capricorn, Earth Element

Magical Tips ★ Promotes the rise of the *kundalini* force. Jet is said to stabilise finances and protect businesses, it can be placed in a cash box or the feng shui wealth corner (far left rear) of one's house or business premises for these purposes.

The most frequently used word in the English language to describe something extremely dark is 'jet', as in 'jet black'. This lustrous and velvety gemstone is a type of black fossilised wood that is actually a variety of hard and compacted coal. It needs enormous pressure when forming.

Jet is almost like a sister stone to amber, in that is not an actual stone (rather, a form of coal called lignite) and can also generate electrical charges when rubbed against wool or silk. In fact, it can be worn with amber to protect you from harmful energies - the amber stores the positive energy, while jet absorbs the discordant vibrations (in fact, jet absorbs negative energies like a sponge so must be cleansed regularly to be effective). Unlike amber, which is resin, jet is driftwood which was compressed under great pressure after being subjected to chemical action in stagnant water. It is also more difficult to obtain than amber, as there is less of it in the world.

Jet has been used as a talisman since Stone Age times, being used in ancient times to protect from 'entities of darkness'. It has long had a reputation as a protective stone, being thought to even possess the power to overcome spells and enchantments. The protective energies of this stone are also believed to keep travellers safe on their journeys, no matter what their mode of transportation.

Jet is a receptive stone and it draws powerful energy and has the ability to both repel negative energy and to transmute it into productive energy, depending on how you personally program it. Used since prehistoric times, it became most well-known during the Victorian era during which it was used for funeral jewellery. This association has lent it the reputation of being helpful during times of grieving, loss and mourning. It is believed to soothe a broken heart linked with the death of a loved one.

As well as being a shielding stone, jet can help you to open your Third Eye chakra and enhance your psychic abilities. As black is associated with the element of spirit or ether, the energy of this gem will help to calm and balance your aura, enabling your extrasensory faculties to express themselves in a safe and calm auric environment; this would be especially beneficial before using the Tarot or other forms of divination.

It is said that those who are attracted to this stone are 'old souls' who have a long experience of being incarnated on the Earth.

Psychologically, jet brings stability, emotional security and balance, promotes control over one's life and circumstances, alleviates depression and balances mood swings. It cleanses the Base chakra and stimulates the rise of the kundalini (life force/sexual energy) force when used in this region.

★ KUNZITE ★

Main Spiritual & Metaphysical Qualities ★ Facilitates self-expression; aligns the Heart, Throat & Third Eye chakras; calms panic attacks & chronic anxiety; emotionally & mentally healing; heals heartache; helps open celestial doorways to aid transitions; facilitates the transfer of knowledge from the higher mind; tranquillising.

Astrological Affinities ★ Aries, Leo, Libra, Scorpio, Air Element

Magical Tips ★ American gemologist G.F. Kunz, kunzite's discoverer, noted kunzite's unique and unusual property of absorbing light and then giving it off when placed in darkness. From this, we can perhaps mystically propose that you can literally see things in a different light when working with this gem.

Vibration ★ High

Discovered in America around 1900 and named after its mineralogist discoverer, Dr G. F. Kunz, kunzite draws much admiration by its flawless transparency and high lustre. Uniquely phosphorescent and with a great sensitivity, its pink-lilac to dark lilac-rose tints add to its appeal. Further, it displays visible flares of a blue-tinged green when viewed from a side angle. Wherever the stunning kunzite occurs, so does another precious crystal: hiddenite.

In crystal healing, kunzite is used to protect the heart and enable it to release emotional blocks in a gentle way. Its soft pink-purple hue has a soothing presence, encouraging a sense of safety and peace. As a stone which has an affinity with the Heart chakra, it exudes love, compassion and peace, and connects us with the unconditional love of the Divine, as it also aligns the Heart with the Throat and Third Eye chakras. This gem comforts and heals the heart on both a physical and emotional level and helps one's heart to awaken after long periods without a meaningful relationship, when trust and opening up have been challenges. In this way, kunzite is a wonderful crystal to have around in the early stages of a new romance, helping one to usher in this new experience with a sense of joy and openness. Worn over the heart, it can attract new love into your life, or indeed simply support you during the first stages of any new relationship.

Kunzite is also a protective stone that provides a shield against negative, unwanted energies; soothing and calming, it is beneficial to people with addictions.

Possessing the power to raise our vibrations, it is a useful stone for meditation that enhances intuition and connects one with the infinite source, thus allowing one to reach a state of higher spiritual awareness.

Ideal for babies and children, kunzite's loving and innocent nature helps them to feel safe and secure. It also has the ability to ease nervous stress, tension and anxiety, and dissolves resistance to new ideas and directions, enabling life to flow and develop in a positive way.

A good balancer on all levels, kunzite promotes emotional equilibrium, enhances self-esteem, encourages tolerance and acceptance, and enables the deeper inner dimensions of the heart to be experienced.

★ KYANITE ★

Astrological Affinities ★ Aries, Taurus, Libra

Magical Tips ★ Kyanite's metaphysical name is 'the sword of truth'. As the seeker of truth it enhances psychic abilities, inner guidance and intuition, and connects the higher mind to the highest frequencies.

Kyanite, also called disthene, is an indigo, translucent blue, white, grey, yellow, black or green-blue stone, which is aligned with the Crown, Third Eye and Throat chakras.

Kyanite is the perfect example of symmetrical elegance, and habitually reminiscent of bluish-grey skies, it has a soft luminosity glowing from its depths. Kyanite grows in flat blade crystals that often have striations (parallel scratches or grooves) along their length, giving this crystal a focused swift action quality that is augmented by these streaks. Kyanite's grooves allow the crystal to move energy quickly between the chakra linkage points, which releases energy blocks, ties, 'hooks' and ensnarements imposed upon one's spirit by other people or negative situations.

Kyanite restores one's energy balance and integrates the body's forces. With conscious attunement it aligns all the chakras and activates their connecting points, balancing and strengthening the subtle bodies. In healing, it stabilises the biomagnetic field after clearing, release, and transformation.

Kyanite strengthens the Throat chakra and its life-force energy can open the way for spiritual healing. It encourages self-expression and speaking one's truth, cutting through ignorance, fears and blockages. It can also facilitate astral or interdimensional travel, enhance creative expression and is particularly useful for meditation, especially if you are having trouble relaxing or clearing the mind.

Kyanite transforms negative thought patterns and opens up the Crown chakra to assist in connecting to your higher self. Calming and tranquillising, this stone promotes clarity and understanding, and with its ability to tune into the 'causal' level, this stone can help spiritual energy manifest in thought and expression.

★ LABRADORITE ★

The Stone of Magic

A man is a bit like a Labrador spar, which has no lustre as you turn it in your hand until you come to a particular angle; then it shows deep and beautiful colours.

Ralph Waldo Emerson

Main Spiritual & Metaphysical Qualities ★ Reduces stress & anxiety; opens spiritual pathways to attune you to your soul's path; spiritually empowering; connects you to the highest Universal energies, allowing you to receive information from the Source; aids expansion; creates an interface to facilitate metaphysical work; enhances perceptive insight, inner knowing & intuitive wisdom; transmutes & banishes fear.

Astrological Affinities ★ Leo, Virgo, Scorpio, Sagittarius, Capricorn, Aquarius, Pisces, Mercury

Magical Tips ★ In every sense, labradorite is a Stone of Magic. It facilitates all alchemical and metaphysical workings. It awakens within you magical abilities, psychic powers and mystical gifts. It is a crystal for shamans, healers, mystics, alchemists and diviners of all kinds, and opens up the doorways and paths leading to enlightenment and Divine connection with the Universe. In Ancient Scandinavia, labradorite was used as an oracle by the indigenous peoples, and it can still be beneficially used for this purpose in this age. The gentle grace of labradorite carries ancient spiritual wisdom at its heart and as such it can answer your questions about your spiritual purpose; it can also connect you with esoteric knowledge, Universal forces, initiation into the 'mysteries', and allow access to the 'Akashic Records' **.

Vibration ★ High

Labradorite Affirmation for Magic ★ "I am open to the mystery of the Universe. I hold in my outer cloudy appearance a rainbow of brilliant hues that can be seen when I am in the light. I am an invitation to take a look at the beauty in your life and to the wonderful things you have created. Even those things that have seemed dark and dreary are now revealed to contain bits of brighter illumination. I am a call to an inward journey. The magic already at work in your life, is becoming visible to you now. Your rainbow will soon rise to the surface."

Labradorite was named in 1770 when discovered in Labrador by missionaries, even though its history goes back for centuries. Labradorite deepens meditation, enhances intuition, and aligns with the Higher Sources.

A member of the feldspar family, labradorite is an opaque deep grey, grey-blue or more ethereal pale grey * stone, possessing a brilliant blue and green sheen displaying rainbow colours. Due to the presence within this mineral of countless minute iron plates, labradorite shows shimmering shades of peacock-blue, green, gold and greenish-yellow, giving it a whole-spectrum colour appearance if viewed from the appropriate angles. Like a dragonfly's wings, the colours appear, then vanish, this optical effect being achieved for the most part by the interference of light in labradorite's physical structure. Indeed, this special quality - labelled 'labradorescence' after the stone itself - makes it one of the most striking and enchanting crystals around. Aside from its blue lustre, glimmers of green, yellow and red may also be seen in some specimens, making labradorite an appealing rainbow-hued stone. When a specimen shows more green labradorescence, it is known as lynx sapphire. White pieces are often sold under the trade name of rainbow moonstone, despite not actually being moonstone, while transparent specimens are often referred to as black moonstone.

Although most aligned with the Third Eye and Crown chakras, labradorite can be used anywhere on the body with equally beneficial effect. Labradorite has a protective power against jealousy, combating negative influences and empowering the Self in times of trouble or doubt. Indeed, it transmutes anything discordant that reaches it, providing a 'screen' for your personal energies, only allowing through that which it discerns is for your higher good. As well as deflecting unwanted energies, labradorite prevents energy leakages from the aura.

Labradorite can help astral projection by strengthening your aura, acting as a 'battery' to give you the energy and confidence to master the process. It also has many other uses as a magical assistant and may help in dream recall, by acting as the 'rainbow bridge' between the conscious and the unconscious minds. It allows for access to prophetic dreams and altered states of reality.

A highly spiritual stone, labradorite is believed to have the power to attract a mentor by raising your vibrational frequency so that you attract helpful guides and beings on both the spiritual and material levels. It can also rise above anything that could sabotage your progress, gently pushing you forward toward your goals, increasing your stamina and encouraging you all the way.

Promoting a synthesis of analytical and rational thought with intuitive, mystical and spiritual wisdom, labradorite is also thought to be a stone of transformation. Therefore, it is a beneficial crystal to use during times of change or transition, imparting strength and perseverance, and facilitating self-growth. Used to stimulate memory, it can be used to treat any disorder affecting the brain.

Labradorite is an excellent meditation stone that can be used to accelerate telepathic abilities and assists communication with your Higher Self. Enhancing intuition and psychic gifts, labradorite bestows the art of 'perfect timing' and energises the imagination and wisdom.

Labradorite will connect you to the corresponding element/s of your surroundings - wearing it to the ocean or a forest, for example, will enhance your connection to Water or Earth energies respectively.

Overall, labradorite is a magical and enchanting stone, a dispeller of darkness, and a bringer of light.

* The pale grey, translucent variety of labradorite gives better results than the darker, opaque types. In the pale grey, light plays more effectively on the stacked crystals within.

** In Eastern mysticism and occultism, the 'Akashic Records' are an all-pervading life principle or all-pervasive space of the cosmos. The akasha is the substance ether, a fifth element and the subtlest of all the elements, and in yoga the akasha is one of three universal principles along with *prana*, the Universal life force, and creative mind. It is said that everything that ever happens throughout the Universe - every emotion, thought, sound, action and so forth - is recorded permanently upon the akasha. The Akashic Records is a term coined in the late nineteenth century, from *akasha*, the Sanskrit word for 'aether', 'space', 'luminous' or 'sky', and is a cosmic compendium of thoughts, emotions and events that exist beyond time and space. The Akashic Record is believed by Theosophists to be a kind of life force which contains information on all that has occurred and all that will occur. These records of past and future events, ideas and actions, are believed to be encoded in a non-physical plane of existence known as the astral plane and were referred to as "indestructible tablets of the astral light" by H.V. Blavatsky, occultist, spirit medium, author and co-founder of the Theosophical Society in 1875.

★ LAPIS LAZULI ★

Main Spiritual & Metaphysical Qualities ★ Transmutes mental & emotional blockages; sets the soul free; encourages expression; facilitates metaphysical insights; spiritually transformative; stimulates psychic abilities; reveals inner truths; alleviates depression; encourages honesty, compassion & truth.

Astrological Affinities ★ Aries, Taurus, Virgo, Libra, Sagittarius, Aquarius, Venus, Jupiter, Air Element

Magical Tips ★ For those wishing to manifest something in their lives, lapis lazuli helps you to focus your energy and amplify it when you're sending it out into the Universe towards a specific goal.

Vibration ★ High

As lapis lazuli does not have a crystalline structure by definition it cannot be referred to as a crystal, but for the purposes of this book, I will refer to it as a crystal or a stone.

Lapis lazuli is a deep royal blue or bluish green mineral whose name, derived from the Latin/Arabic word *lazward*, meaning blue, refers to its striking colouration. The later Latin form *lazurius* and the French word *azure* are also linked with this stone's very unique shade of blue. In fact, it can be taken quite literally to mean 'sky stone', from the Latin *lapis* meaning 'stone' and the Persian *lazward* meaning 'blue' or 'sky'. When polished it displays sparkling metallic flecks that are due to particles of iron pyrite within its matrix.

Ancient manuscripts reveal that this gem was considered the sapphire of Ancient Greece, being described as a 'sapphire sprinkled with gold dust'. Centuries ago, these sparkles in the deep blue of the polished stone were compared to the twinkling of the stars in the heavenly firmament, and it was hence called the Heavenly Stone. Indeed, this is an ancient stone that can be traced back to Mesopotamian and Egyptian civilisations.

Lapis lazuli is said to be a stone of truth, encouraging verbal integrity and honesty of the spirit. Stimulating the Third Eye and balancing the Throat chakra, lapis enhances enlightenment, inspires confidence so one can express their emotions more easily, connects the physical to the astral plane, links one with the source of omnipotence, reveals inner truths, increases vitality, eases depression, and facilitates spiritual ascension. As such, it stimulates enlightenment, psychic abilities, spiritual journeying, and mystical powers. Shielding the wearer during the process of spiritual development, it also allows the wearer to draw wisdom from natural sources. Bringing objectivity and clarity, it assists in discrimination, active listening, receptivity, comprehension, and other functions of the higher mind. It harmonises the physical, emotional, mental and spiritual levels of the being. This balancing brings with it a deep sense of inner self-knowing and connection.

Overall, lapis lazuli reveals our inner 'voice', encourages self-awareness, and allows for uninhibited self-expression. It brings the enduring qualities of honesty, compassion and truth. A powerful thought amplifier, lapis encourages creativity through connection and attunement to 'the Source'.

Possessing enormous serenity, lapis lazuli releases stress, alleviates insomnia, and brings a deep sense of peace. It is a protective stone that enables contact with our ethereal guardians; indeed, it is a special key for spiritual ascension. As it is a stone of great power, lapis should be worn with care if you are unfamiliar with its spirituality. This is because it can transform you into a channel for an abundance of energy to flow through but is also the reason why it is so beloved by psychics and mediums. Because of its power and intensity, the wearer needs to be *ready* to act as this channel; if unready or unprepared, it can prove too intense for the uninitiated. Similarly, it should also not be worn for long periods at a time, not even all day, because such is its strength that it can elevate the higher senses until a receptive owner may want nothing else but its refining energy, leaving no thought for the body which houses the soul and spirit. Physically, lapis is a fine transmitter of energy in the hands of a sensitive crystal therapist 'channelling' health and wellbeing to a patient.

So many healing virtues are attributed to this stone that it is difficult to specify the most important, but lapis can be defined as an overall emotional sanctuary.

Ultimately, it helps you to confront truth, however and in whatever form you find it, and to accept what that truth's message may teach. A saying of the ancient Sumerian priests was: "He who carries with him into battle an amulet of Lapis carries with him the presence of his god." In regards to this powerfully-charged gem, this perhaps encapsulates all.

★ MAGNETITE ★

Main Spiritual & Metaphysical Qualities ★ Grounds; energises; enhances positive mood states.

Astrological Affinities ★ Aries, Virgo, Scorpio, Capricorn, Aquarius, Mars, Earth Element

Magical Tips ★ To attract something into your life, obtain a piece of magnetite (or better still, a pair of lodestones) and consecrate it with the four elements, then carry the consecrated stone in a small pouch of the colour that corresponds to your wish (e.g. green for money, red for luck, blue for healing, pink for love, orange for happiness.)

A metallic iron ore stone that is also known as 'lodestone', the most common use of magnetite as a charm is to attract things to you. As magnetite is magnetic, it is believed to attract love, loyalty and commitment. The Chinese call it 't' su shi', meaning 'the loving stone'. This crystal is renowned for its magnetic attraction to iron and also for pointing to the north and south poles when hung from a thread. It has a powerful positive-negative polarity and is extremely useful in magnetic therapy, working with the body's own biomagnetic field and meridians, and with that of the planet in deep Earth-healing.

Magnetite acts as a grounding stone and connects the Base and Earth chakras to the nurturing energies of the ground beneath us, which sustain the life force and vitality of the physical body.

Magnetite will attract and repel, energise and sedate, clear and build, and also aids telepathy, meditation and visualisation. It enhances a balanced perspective and trust in your own intuitive wisdom. Emotionally, it can be used to alleviate negative feeling forms such as grief, anger, fear, anxiety, and over-attachment, and usher in more positive mood states. Magnetite assists in the release of emotional trauma and gently but firmly pushes you towards change. It dissolves fear and reluctance around change while simultaneously protecting you and helping you to grow.

Magnetite also helps to bring the intellect into harmony with the emotions in order to cultivate inner stability. Overall, magnetite is both grounding and energising, and aligns our subtle energy systems with the Earth's magnetic field, bringing security, strength, sustenance, restoration, and life-force renewal. Magnetite has a hardness of 5.5, aligning it with Mercury's number. **

** Magnetite is best placed next to the body rather than directly upon it, to avoid the body absorbing too much of its energies which may be toxic if overused. Likewise, when handling magnetite, hold it in a tissue or cloth.

★ MALACHITE ★ ★

Main Spiritual & Metaphysical Qualities ★ Powerfully transformative; spiritual evolution; karmic & soul cleanser; activates one's soul purpose; heals grief; releases toxic emotions; eases heartache; soothes emotions; facilitates explorative journeys & takes one deep inside the self; potent overall healer.

Astrological Affinities ★ Aries, Taurus, Libra, Scorpio, Sagittarius, Capricorn, Venus, Earth Element

Magical Tips ★ A powerful stone of intense inner transformation and soul catharsis, malachite is perhaps best used under the guidance of an experienced crystal worker.

Vibration ★ Deep & Earthy

Malachite is a striking, rich-green layered opaque stone of intense energy. Its dramatic patterns echo its versatile and vast healing qualities. It is so named because its layers resemble the soft green of the marshmallow plant, derived from the Greek word for the plant's colouring - *malache*.

Malachite is connected with the Solar Plexus, Throat and Heart chakras, and although powerful and probing, it will increase courage and determination, dissolving fear and anxiety, and help you break free from limitations.

Malachite is a copper-rich crystal which can be used diagnostically to get to the heart of a problem. It is a stone of balance that soothes, but also strengthens, the nervous system. A resolute stone that draws insights out from deep within the subconscious mind and facilitates the regeneration of the Self, with dedicated use, this intense stone can balance and bring harmony to the body and psyche. Malachite is an exceptionally evolving ** stone that is perfect for all self-transformational explorations, and the more you work with it, the more expansive its influence becomes. It illuminates the darker corners of the mind, and in doing so demands that you examine the deep-rooted causes of any physical or mental issues. This is also a stone of alignment and is excellent to use in self-exploration journeys. Working with malachite ultimately helps you confront whatever it is that is blocking your spiritual unfoldment and wellbeing. It also has a detoxifying effect, cleansing the body of both physical and emotional impurities.

Assisting in the release of outworn or restrictive patterns of thought or behaviour, malachite is both physically and psychologically vitalising. It also facilitates release and letting go, enabling you to move forward. Used in combination with other similarly acting crystals, malachite can heal grief, ease heartache, draw out toxic emotions, break unwanted ties, root out psychosomatic causes of bodily dis-ease, and teach you how to take responsibility for your thoughts, actions and feelings.

Malachite is known as the 'sleep stone' because it has the effect of inducing drowsiness if gazed at for long enough. Indeed, it can ease insomnia, improve quality of sleep and dreaming, and offer protection from nightmares. Indeed, malachite is used for its protective properties as well. It absorbs pollutants and negative energies, picking them up from the atmosphere, the physical body and the aura. It guards against radiation of all kinds and soaks up plutonium pollution. It also clears electromagnetic pollution and heals any discordant Earth energies.

In magic and divination, malachite can be used for scrying - journeying through its convoluted patterns can stimulate images and assist in receiving insights or messages from the future. It is regarded as "the mirror of the soul" and so some crystal experts may advise against wearing malachite as it may prove too powerful and confronting for some. Essentially though, it is a true empowerment crystal, which helps you reclaim your power by bringing to the surface any hidden issues, toxic thoughts or repressed feelings that are holding you back. If this stone had an expression, it would be, "I Am." It will help those who are brave enough to work with it, to step into their true power.

As a stone of transformation and change, life is lived more intensely and adventurously under the influence of this vivid gem. Malachite will enhance spiritual rebirth and growth, and when placed on the Solar Plexus it will facilitate deep emotional healing, allowing one's deepest self to shift in a new, positive direction. This profound crystal will surprise you with its merciless spotlight on what has held you back for so long - and will further astound with the depth of transmutation that you can achieve with this knowledge.

* Malachite will lose its sheen if cleansed in salt water - smudging this crystal with sandalwood or sage incense is preferable. It should be cleansed before and after use by placing it on a quartz cluster in the Sun. Also, malachite needs to be handled with caution and is best used under the supervision of a qualified crystal therapist. Always use malachite in its polished form and wash your hands thoroughly after handling.

** It is believed by some people that malachite is still evolving and will be one of the most important healing stones in years to come.

★ MERLINITE ★

Main Spiritual & Metaphysical Qualities ★ Balances the mind, body & spirit; brings masculine & feminine energies into alignment; realigns neurotransmitters to accommodate expanded vibrational energy; connects one to soul destiny & the Akashic Record *.

Astrological Affinities ★ Sagittarius, Pisces

Magical Tips ★ Merlinite is a Stone of Magic and self-mastery. This crystal was named after the wizard Merlin, because of its specific attributes of attracting magical and mystical experiences into your life. This stone is especially used for this very purpose, to amplify the magic in your life. As well as these properties, merlinite's greatest gift is karmic healing.

Vibration ★ High

Essentially, merlinite teaches us the fundamentals of mysticism. It is a stone of duality - of black and white, of masculine and feminine, of light and dark. Merlinite attracts powerful energy and good luck into your life, and it may also take you to places where you make contact with the deeper, unhealed parts of yourself. It can impart the courage to confront these parts of your shadowy self and consciously integrate them.

The vibration of this stone is very shamanistic, as it allows you to access the energy of the natural world and communicate with elementals. Blending heavenly and earthly energies, Merlinite connects one to all the other elemental forces - Earth, Water, Wind, Fire, Spirit, and Storm. It is also said to conjure ancient memories of wizards and alchemists of times past, and stimulates deep intuition, psychic knowing, and spiritual mediumship.

An intense stone that aids the birth of creativity and clear psychic visions, merlinite will assist you to access your higher spiritual energy, and to make contact with guides, mentors, angels and teachers in the ethereal realms.

Opening your energy fields, merlinite has an innate capacity to serve as a channel for manifestation. Overall, it stimulates magic, synchronicities, mediumship, past life recall, deep intuition, shamanic journeying, and spiritual communication, and powerfully reminds one that the Spirit is eternal and lasts beyond the physical.

* The *Akasha*, Sanskrit meaning 'cosmic sky', is a non-physical plane of existence where all human history is encoded. In scientific thought, the

connectivity hypothesis speaks of the existence of a subquantum energy field in which everything that happens is holographically and permanently recorded. Quantum physics suggests that future possibilities are also encoded in and etched into this field. Moments of great personal and collective emotional trauma and soul dramas make the biggest impression on the Record.

★ MOLDAVITE ★

Main Spiritual & Metaphysical Qualities ★ Transformative; carrier of cosmic wisdom; connects one to the highest planes of consciousness & the cosmos

Astrological Affinities ★ Taurus, Libra, Capricorn, Venus, Neptune

Magical Tips ★ In magical work, moldavite is useful for inter-dimensional travel, spiritual ascension and aids in all things relating to the higher spiritual planes. Its key words are transformation, rapid mystical evolution, chakra activation, cleansing, protection, ascension of the heart, and the increased incidence of synchronicities.

Vibration ★ High

A member of the Tektite group, with a hardness of 5.5 to 6, the colour of moldavite is usually a deep forest green. Regarded as a 'new age' stone, moldavite can elevate the consciousness and activate your higher self. It is connected with all the chakras, but particularly resonates with the Heart, Third Eye and Crown.

Believed to be a powerful carrier of cosmic wisdom, moldavite can help connect you with higher guidance, star beings, ascended masters, and astral intelligence. A stone of karmic and soul transformation, moldavite can help connect you to and access the Akashic Records, an ethereal plane upon which everything in the Universe is encoded. In doing so, it can help take you back to your past to reconnect with your inherent wisdom and soul purpose.

A powerful meditative aid, moldavite also has the ability to enhance, accelerate and amplify the beneficial effects of other stones it comes into contact with.

★ MOONSTONE ★

Main Spiritual & Metaphysical Qualities ★ Promotes clairvoyance & deep meditation; alleviates apathy; increases concentration; confers a sense of serenity & equilibrium.

Astrological Affinities ★ Cancer, Libra, Scorpio, Pisces, Water Element

Magical Tips ★ Moonstone opens the mind to hoping and wishing, inspiration and impulse, magic and enchantment. It grants intuitive recognition and even flashes of insight and allows one to absorb what is needed from the Universe.

An opalescent form of feldspar, resembling in its colour the pale lustrous gleam of moonlight, this is traditionally regarded as a stone of the Goddess and is sacred to all things Lunar and celestial.

Moonstone is an ethereal, translucent, milky stone, which occurs in yellow, peach, grey, white, blue and colourless. The beautiful sheen of this stone seems to wax and wane like its namesake and the crystal has featured in much Lunar folklore, being considered a sacred link to the Moon in many cultures.

Moonstone is believed to absorb the rays of the Moon, and with them some of the mystical attributes of that heavenly body. Its potency is said to increase as the Moon waxes (or goes from New to Full) and lessens when that orb declines. Moonstone is a symbol of hope and a stone of new beginnings. Like the Moon, this stone is reflective and reminds us that, as the Moon waxes and wanes, so too is everything a part of a cycle of change. Its most powerful effect is that of calming the emotions, and it is also useful in honing one's intuition and improving natural psychic abilities. It is also a stone of wishes and for working towards goal manifestation.

Moonstone can offer clarity and perspective about your place in the world, and your true path, like looking down upon your own personal world from the distance of the Moon. Possessing a gentle nature which promotes kindness and peace, it is calming, balancing, soothing, healing, protective and uplifting, particularly to those whose Moon is strong in their astrological chart. Moonstone improves emotional intelligence and provides deep healing within this realm. It is believed to have the power to endow love, wealth and wisdom.

This enchanting gem helps to identify emotional patterns that are stored in the subconscious mind and can act as a guardian. Moonstone also helps calm emotional fears surrounding love and relationships. If you have fear around being in love or being hurt by it, moonstone can help you transcend that; it will soften a hard heart and allow you to feel safe.

Being of the Lunar rays, moonstone makes conscious the unconscious and promotes and enhances empathy, lucidity, clairvoyance, receptivity, serendipity and synchronicity - however, regarding these last two, care needs to be taken that it does not induce illusions in response to wishful thinking. It is helpful in times of shock, possessing a calm, flowing peace that helps restore emotional balance in everyday experiences too, and is an excellent aid for fertility, as it can help you to manifest and sustain a healthy pregnancy.

Moonstone is one of the traditional birthstones of June and resonates most strongly with the sign of Cancer.

Adularia Moonstone ★ Probably the most precious variety of moonstone is adularia, which echoes the Moon's pearly sheen. Named after its place of discovery in Adula, Switzerland, this gem has a soft luminous glow. When cut in domed shapes a hovering line of light dances across its surface giving the illusion of being above the crystal, rather than coming from the fine, fibrous particles within, lending it an aura of illusion and magic.

★ MORGANITE ★

Main Spiritual & Metaphysical Qualities ★ Helpful for girls entering puberty who do not have a mother; opens communication channels with guardian angels & spirit guides; encourages the expression of emotional needs; promotes compassion, unconditional love & forgiveness; instils gentle personal power & grace.

Astrological Affinities ★ Taurus, Libra, Pisces, Venus

Magical Tips ★ Place morganite on your Heart chakra to gently bring repressed emotions, traumas and feelings to the surface so they can be released. It can enlighten you as to what your soul needs to move forward and love more fully.

Vibration ★ High

A member of the beryl family, Morganite is a lovely soft pink semi-precious gemstone which activates, opens, balances and cleanses the Heart chakra. It clears, harmonises and heals this energy centre, releasing fear, resentment and anger, and assists in recognising unfulfilled emotional needs and feelings which have gone unexpressed. It can also reveal defence-mechanisms which are fear-based making meaningful relationships difficult, thereby creating resistance to healing and transformation. Further, it stabilises the emotional field and brings wisdom and calmness of mind. It increases the ability to accept loving words and actions from others, and releases attachments to old relationships that have ended badly or need resolution, encouraging one to move forward with renewed purpose and an open heart.

Emitting a loving pink ray, morganite promotes abundance of the heart and the prosperity of love. Used to attract and maintain love, it is a powerful, high vibrational, Universal stone of unconditional love. It helps to lighten the burdens of the heart and to align you with your Divine Plan. It encourages loving thoughts and actions, compassion, empathy, self-control, consideration, patience, responsibility, and receptiveness to others.

Morganite inspires joy and reverence for life and increases the opportunities through which you can experience the unconditional love of the Divine in its highest and purest form. Morganite is a crystal that assists us to vibrate with the power of heightened feminine energy. As such, it is a potent support for women, enabling them to feel and live through their own strength and beauty, radiating outward from deep within. Because of its connection to the Divine energies, morganite may also be used to cultivate peace and acceptance when dealing with deep loss and grief.

Ultimately, as a powerful stone of love and the heart centre, morganite is a remarkable stone for attracting one's soul mate or for deepening a current relationship.

★ MOSS AGATE ★

Main Spiritual & Metaphysical Qualities ★ Mentally stabilising & strengthening; enhances connection & communication with the plant, animal & devic kingdoms; releases fear; good for new beginnings.

Astrological Affinities ★ Taurus, Cancer, Virgo, Libra

Magical Tips ★ Moss agate is a stone of new beginnings, so is excellent for starting new projects and for attracting abundance into your experience if there have been blocks to receiving in the past. Moss agate is believed to be connected with agricultural nature spirits and devas and can provide a link between the plant and mineral kingdoms, allowing you to communicate with both to bring forth fertility, bounty or the Earth's wealth (traditionally moss agate was believed to bring rain, ensuring the right amount fell for crops to flourish).

Vibration ★ Earthy

Moss agate is an enchanting stone which contains dark green or blackish-green patterns imitative of ferns and moss against a creamy translucent or clear background. Moss agate, like all green stones, contains the energies of nature which are nurturing and balancing to the subtle energy systems. Green crystals can also promote feelings of freedom and space and be used to release fear and remove 'tightness' that can become overwhelming when you feel trapped by inharmonious relationships or circumstances.

Moss agate is often referred to as the 'gardener's stone' and is said to be helpful to farmers in ensuring a good crop by way of encouraging rain, abundance, fertility and protection of the Earth, and helping one communicate more effectively with animals and plants. Moss agate provides a link between the plant and mineral kingdoms, assisting in communicating with the natural world and nature spirits. It is also attributed to attracting and enhancing prosperity, success, healing, restoration, confidence, strength and creativity.

Moss agate is a stabilising stone and is refreshing to the soul, helping you to see beauty in all you do or behold. It is a very lucky omen for the gradual growth of what you currently most need in your life, whether it be money, recognition, promotion, health or love. As a stone of wealth, it also attracts abundance and encourages trust, optimism and hope in the Earth's and the Universe's gifts.

A crystal of new beginnings and growth or regrowth of trust, moss agate can be used to release old fears and restore a sense of connection with the world after a period of disenchantment or disillusionment.

Moss agate aligns with the Heart chakra and is a powerful mental and physical healer, working on emotional thinking patterns that manifest in dis-ease, helping to clear those patterns so that health can prevail.

Releasing fear and deep-rooted stress, moss agate improves self-esteem and highlights positive personality traits. It is also believed that moss agate is beneficial when fostering new friendships or seeking a compatible lover.

★ OBSIDIAN ★

Main Spiritual & Metaphysical Qualities ★ Facilitates spiritual change; re-empowers the self; goes deep into the subconscious & mirrors your inner being; absorbs negative energies; confers humility; eases bewilderment; stabilises emotions; encourages just behaviour; protects from danger; may promote emotional catharsises; encourages deep soul-healing; realigns you with your spiritual path; reveals the inner beauty hidden in the recesses of the soul.

Astrological Affinities ★ Depending on colour, all zodiac signs, Fire Element

Magical Tips ★ This 'jewel of the volcano' has been used in magical ceremonies and ritual for thousands of years. Highly polished obsidian oracle mirrors were used by the Mayans and Aztecs to divine the future. Regarded as a mystical portal between time and space, obsidian crystal balls and mirrors have been used since antiquity as a shamanic and divinatory tool.

Vibration ★ Earthy

Obsidian is named after its discoverer, Obsius. Not strictly speaking a mineral, obsidian is actually a natural glass once spewed from an erupting volcano. It is essentially molten lava that cooled so quickly it had no time for facets to form or to crystallise.

Obsidian is a dark, glassy, non-crystalline rock of volcanic origin and is hence found in places of such activity, such as Hawaii, Japan and Iceland. It is also mined in Mexico, Guatemala, Ecuador and the USA, where it can be found in solid, glassy blocks known as 'apache tears'. Apache tear is believed to especially relieve grief, mourning and sorrow. Balancing to one's emotional state, this form of obsidian assists in releasing negative emotions. Apache tear is an effective and powerful grounding stone.

Obsidian is usually black, but it comes in a variety of other colours, such as red, brown, blue, green, rainbow, red-black, silver, purple, mahogany, and tinted with a silver- or gold-sheen. If it has lacy white flecks, it is called snowflake obsidian, which is also known as 'the temperance stone'.

Mahogany obsidian is said to enhance meditation, increase self-esteem, impart vital strength and energy, and help to combat depression and sadness.

This material, which is usually black, sometimes contains white and grey markings which have given rise to such descriptive names as the already mentioned 'snowflake', 'apache tears', and 'flowering'.

Both the Aztecs and the Mayans used obsidians extensively - indeed, obsidian is easily broken into sharp-edged pieces or 'flakes', and in the absence of iron this was those civilisations' main cutting tool.

Also called the 'wizard stone', black obsidian has magical associations. Spiritually, obsidian vitalises soul purpose and stimulates growth on all levels. It urges exploration of the unknown and opens up new horizons by eliminating energy blockages. It assists in helping you to know who you truly are, by compelling you to confront your shadow self and identify behavioural patterns that may be hindering you. Obsidian is a fierce, protective stone that helps to unlock the unconscious and make room for this shadow self to come forward and communicate. In fact, nothing can be hidden from obsidian. It has been described as the 'warrior of truth' that draws hidden imbalances to the surface to release them. Working extremely fast and with great power, it is truth-enhancing and merciless, exposing flaws, weaknesses, and blockages. With its reflective qualities (many scrying balls * and magic mirrors are made from it), it challenges us to search deep within. In this way, it is best used under the guidance of a qualified crystal therapist as it may bring up negative emotions and unpleasant truths, but under skilful and careful supervision, its cathartic properties are invaluable, helping us to recognise conditions that disempower us.

As a truth-bringer, it impels us to grow and provides support while we do so, forming a shield against negativity, strengthening us in times of need. Helpful for healers and highly sensitive people, obsidian blocks psychic attack and removes discordant spiritual influences. As obsidian is so effective at soaking up negative energies, it is essential to clean the stone under running water after each time it has been used for this purpose.

Divinatory stones made from obsidian are an excellent aid in foreseeing possible outcomes of the future or a particular situation.

Obsidian, particularly the darker varieties, has a particular affinity with the Base chakra and is an excellent stone for grounding and anchoring us firmly to Mother Earth, making us feel stable, secure, assured, and balanced. Obsidian is also beneficial when used to bring out your 'inner warrior'. If you are feeling particularly nervous about an event or a situation, holding a piece of obsidian can allows its strength to radiate through you.

* Crystal gazing - or scrying - using a sphere of clear quartz or obsidian is an ancient way of moving beyond the confines of the rational mind to gain information and insights that otherwise would not be available to one. Scrying makes intensive and extensive use of your intuition and perception of subtle-energy impressions. Recognising these subtle-energy impressions is also helped by using deep blue or indigo crystals during meditation experiences.

★ ONYX ~ BLACK ★

Main Spiritual & Metaphysical Qualities ★ Encourages positive thinking; helps concentration; eliminates negative thought patterns; assists memory; brings calm & inner peace; helps to combat unfounded fears; promotes good humour & laughter; tones & strengthens; brings clarity by alleviating confusion; imparts a sense of security & courage.

Astrological Affinities ★ Cancer, Leo, Aquarius, Capricorn, Saturn, Earth Element

Magical Tips ★ Onyx is well known for its use as a protective amulet and is helpful in times where you may encounter discordant influences, hostility or unpleasant people or environments.

Onyx is a type of agate of various colours, sometimes black or white. Deriving its name from the Arabic 'el jaza' means sadness, onyx used to have a bad reputation as it was thought to make people pessimistic, lonely and sad, but amongst the virtues ascribed to it were those of protection - through avoiding conflicts, adversity and tragedy - and that of bringing patience and wisdom to those who wore it. Onyx is a grounding stone which has the ability to manipulate energy. It can be protective but can also be used for more sinister purposes. It is ultimately a giver of strength and can restore depleted energies that have been taken from you.

Onyx's properties are earthy and cooling, and it is well-suited to the energies of its planetary ruler, Saturn, which governs order, discipline and structure. Saturn lends these qualities to onyx and therefore the stone's grounding nature makes it a good aid for resolving matters that require solidity, the courage of one's convictions, and determination. Because it absorbs negative energies however, it is important to cleanse this crystal after use, to avoid holding the unfavourable vibrations it has absorbed.

★ OPAL ★

Hold your opal, focus your attention into the crystal, and visualise what you wish to manifest. It will
come into being.

Judy Hall

Main Spiritual & Metaphysical Qualities ★ Instils hope, innocence & purity; aids manifestation; strengthens the power of thought; brings inspiration, imagination & creativity; allows for transformation by bringing to light your inner truth; healing, balancing & energising to all chakras.

Astrological Affinities ★ Gemini, Cancer, Virgo, Libra, Scorpio, Pisces, the Moon, Mercury, Air Element

Magical Tips ★ Opal is considered capable of opening up the Third Eye and Crown chakras, and above other minerals is used by many mystics to lead them into supernatural and otherworldly realms. In Greco-Roman times, opal was associated with Mercury/Hermes, and through this power could see into their realms. It was believed that holding an opal in your left hand and gazing into its depths would bring to you all that you desired. Opal combines the water and emotions with the fire of sudden change and can thus be a stone of amazing transformation, assisting you to heal old emotions that may be holding you back and put the fire back into you to get things moving again. It eases the process of change. This is a stone of ascension and connection with the Ascended Masters.

Vibration ★ Earthy to High

Opal is an ethereal and delicate stone with a fine vibration, reminding us of the wondrous unfolding of the Divine Universe. Known as the Queen of Gems, it is one of the most beautiful stones and has been highly prized for thousands of years.

As opal contains all the colours of the other stones, it can be used to amplify all other crystals' energies. Unlike most other gemstones, opal is not crystalline in form, but rather is defined as a mineraloid. It is an amorphous silica variety of quartz, is comparatively soft, and owes its beauty to the wonderful play of colour from its surface. This mineral is formed from the shells or skeletons of very tiny plant and animal organisms, and occurs in many different colours and varieties, such as fire opal, girasol quartz, moss opal, milk opal, precious opal and resin opal, among others.

Bringing miraculous order to a vast array of patterns and colours, the opal unites heaven and Earth in an intricate union of Water and Fire. The characteristically iridescent, rainbow hues of the gem are caused by irregular refraction of light from its surface, which is traversed by innumerable tiny cracks. In the process of its formation, the surface becomes covered by these cracks, and these crevices become filled in with a substance containing more or less water than the surrounding surface. The great irregularities, refractions and play of colour varies according to the angle from which the gem is viewed: blue, perhaps when looked at in one direction, yellow or crimson if we view it from another.

Opals have always generated strong passions, according to the folklore of many cultures. In Ancient Egypt and Babylon, opals were considered a powerful healing gem, combining the qualities of Fire and Water, and were said to bring good luck. Opal was also sacred to medieval England, Greece and some Arabic societies.

Opal is said to improve vitality by magnifying energy, enhance one's self-image, and improve one's fortune or luck. It has protective powers, stimulates cosmic consciousness and induces psychic visions. Absorbent and reflective, on a spiritual level opal picks up thoughts and feelings, amplifies them, and returns them to Source. A protective and karmic stone, it teaches that what you put out comes back.

An excellent aid for transformation, opal enhances self-worth and helps you understand your full potential. It stimulates originality and dynamic creativity and encourages an interest in the arts. Opal is also associated with desire and eroticism, love and passion; it is a seductive stone that intensifies emotional states and dissolves inhibitions. It can also help you gain access to your true self, magnifying your personality traits and bringing them to the surface for healing.

Overall, opal works well with the emotional, mental, spiritual and etheric bodies, as well as balancing all the chakras, particularly the higher ones.

Overall, opal is a magical gem carrying all the colour and beauty of the rainbow, and its magic essence is just as ephemeral - not quite graspable, but still within reach. Opal can provide a much-needed burst of energy, boost self-confidence, enhance creativity and intuition, help release anger, and connect you to your Higher Self.

* Opal contains more water than any other mineral, up to 21 per cent, and is porous, so it should not be immersed in water or brought into contact with oils, as these may harm or destroy it.

★ OPAL ~ BLACK ★

Black opal is a delicate yet powerful mineral with a fine vibration, which enhances cosmic consciousness and induces psychic and mystical visions. The ancients believed the opal was the mineral bridge between heaven and Earth, for which reason they sometimes labelled it 'The Eye of the Universe'. Even more significantly it was, and still is, 'The Stone of Hope'.

Until recently, the only black opals in the world came from a nine-square mile area in New South Wales, Australia, called Lightning Ridge. Now top grade stones have been discovered in Indonesia, where they cost less because their potential market value is less well understood. Both occurrences yield a semi-black opal as well, but the Indonesian 'Java Black', with its flashing, iridescent 'fire' - a range of colours covering the whole spectrum set against a brilliantly jet-black background - is a particularly appealing gem. Black opal resonates with the Base and Sacral chakras and the reproductive organs, making it particularly useful for releasing sexual tension or repression that arise from an emotional cause. It is also a good stone to use for processing and integrating newly freed emotions.

Like all black stones, black opal is useful for grounding, emotional security and alleviating negative feeling states by clearing energy blockages. Its focus is to clear and build. Black opal, like other opals, is also excellent for enhancing creativity and intuition, and connection to your Higher Path.

★ PEARL ★

The graceful movements come from a pearl somewhere on the ocean floor.

Rumi

Main Spiritual & Metaphysical Qualities ★ Symbolises honesty, truth, purity & love; amplifies feeling states (positive & negative).

Astrological Affinities ★ Cancer, Scorpio, Pisces, Venus, the Moon, Water Element

Magical Tips ★ Pearl can be used to attract wealth. In Indian mythology, pearl is known as the 'Mother Gem of the Sea', and is sacred to Lakshmi, the goddess of wealth. A spell to bring new fortune into one's life draws upon this legendary connection: the ritual involved throwing a small pearl that you have recently bought into a stream during the waxing Moon phase. The principle of this spell is that giving up something of value will draw more wealth into your life, and that by casting the jewel away, you have belief in your own power to attract the prosperity you desire.

Pearls have a long, well-documented and distinguished history. Pearl is formed within bivalve mollusc shells and there are four types of this jewel * - in order of value from the most expensive, they are: spherical, pear-shaped, button-shaped and irregular (baroque). Pearl is usually white, tinged with colours such as cream, yellow, pink, green, black, blue or brown. Coloured pearl is more valuable, such as the pink, bronze and black (the rarest and most expensive) varieties.

Pearls are linked with water and the Moon, and are symbols of spiritual wisdom, purity, and hidden archaic knowledge. As an emblem of innocence and peace, the pearl was once thought to be sacred to the Moon and the goddess of young women, Diana. In Ancient Greece, the pearl was worn by the goddess Aphrodite and their culture regarded pearls as a symbol of love, marriage and union. Aphrodite and Venus, the Roman goddess of love, were both known as 'Lady of the Pearls'.

According to some traditions, pearls are said to have aphrodisiac qualities if they are worn as charms, and powdered pearls are still used in some Eastern medicine systems to produce powerful love potions. Used medicinally, the pearl has been used to treat a number of physical ailments throughout the ages. In modern medicine, pearls that are rejected as gems are processed and ground to a fine powder, providing the pharmaceutical industry a valuable source of calcium, and the cosmetic industry an ingredient for face powders, creams and potions.

The beauty of pearls have seen them prized as a symbol of purity and love for centuries, and they can be worn to promote honesty if you wish to remain true to yourself in all that you do. Pearls are also useful for releasing your past and letting go of ideas that are no longer serving you. In doing this, you are also in a better position to reassess your beliefs and current opinions, and to re-evaluate what is holding you back from achieving your true potential. Pearls are essentially a useful gemstone to work with if you are at a crossroads and needing to solidify your views with more harmonious energies in order to move forward.

It is worth noting that pearls reflect and amplify the energy of the wearer, so if you are feeling down on yourself, they shouldn't be worn. However, if you are feeling positive about yourself, wearing pearls will amplify this and enhance your attractiveness, which may help draw new romance into your life, hence their well-known use as a 'love charm'.

Pearls are sensitive, like their Cancerian companions, and relatively soft, with a Mohs scale hardness of only 3 to 4. Indeed, they will dissolve in certain conditions, so should never be immersed in any acidic liquids. They should also never be kept in a warm place, as they are made up of two per cent water, and warmth may cause them to dry out or to develop cracks and fissures. However, despite its fragile physical nature, the pearl's legendary beauty endures. Diamond has been known for centuries as the King of Gems, due to its stunning sparkle and invincible structure; but the pearl is rightly considered the Queen, for its pure radiant beauty.

Mother of Pearl ★ Mother of pearl is the beautiful, shimmering, smooth inner lining found in shells such as pearl oysters and abalone. These luminescent shells can be used in magical workings for enhancing existing relationships, protecting the home, and to attract new friendships.

* There are said to be four or five varieties of oyster pearl, which all differ according to the element that influenced their formation. This might be one of the four classical ones of Water, Air, Earth and Fire, plus the Vedic fifth, *akasha*, which encompasses all of them and constitutes the material support of the world. If it is Water, the pearl will be very lustrous - a brilliant, white, the delicate play of colours on its surface capturing the shimmering of flowing water. If the influence comes from Air, it will be blue-toned, and reflect the light shining on it. Pearls influence by Fire will have a pink, sometimes almost red, tone, and will emit reddish glimmers of light. If the influencing element is Earth, the pearl will have a much heavier appearance and be coarser than the others. Pearls influenced by *akasha* will lack lustre and be very light in shade.

* For many the production and cultivation of pearls may be considered an ethical issue, for as many as 50 per cent of pearl oysters may die in the process of being suspended in ocean cages for pearl-production. If you are concerned about the moral side of pearl farming, it would be wise to know where you are sourcing your gems from, and their ethical standards and practices.

★ PERIDOT ★

Main Spiritual & Metaphysical Qualities ★ Manifestation; encourages the gift of premonition; promotes insight; calms the emotions & the troubled minds of the mentally ill; transmutes negative thought patterns; helps one to access the wisdom of the higher mind; instils confidence; encourages forgiveness.

Astrological Affinities ★ Leo, Virgo, Libra, Scorpio, Capricorn, Pisces, the Sun

Magical Tips ★ A light green gem, chrysolite is a type of peridot and is associated with the Sun, symbolising power, wealth and triumph. The magician Agrippa said that a peridot held to the Sun "shines forth a golden star." In magical practice, peridot can be placed on each point of a five-pointed star in any form, and what you most wish to manifest can be visualised, then released into the ether for manifestation.

Vibration ★ Earthy to High

Peridot is an attractive crystal belonging to the olivine family, and displays a charming range of greens, from pale to dramatic. The deep olive green coloured peridot, has yellow lights radiating from its depths and is completely transparent, albeit sometimes with a slightly cloudy surface.

Peridot is an unusual stone in that it is the only gem found in meteorites. In ancient times, peridot was revered as a stone of purity that protected against negative energies. The pharaohs of ancient Egypt considered peridot to be the property of their gods, and it was traditionally used to keep evil spirits away. Greatly respected by the Egyptians, peridot was called the "gem of the Sun." It is still considered, and used as, a protective stone and is beneficial to the aura. A power cleanser and tonic, it releases and neutralises toxins on all levels and purifies the mind and body.

Peridot opens, cleanses and activates the Heart and Solar Plexus chakras and clears burdens, bitterness, greed, guilt, jealousies, obsessions, unhelpful thoughts, and 'baggage'.

Peridot works well as an inspirational stone. When you feel stuck or blocked in a situation, use this crystal to help give you a fresh angle or insight into the solution. Peridot assists you to move forward, detach yourself from discordant outside forces, and encourages you to look to your own higher energies for spiritual guidance.

An effective mind-sharpener, peridot aids in learning how to forgive yourself and to step forth and take responsibility for your own life. It enhances confidence and assertion, and alleviates resentment, envy, anger, spite and hurts from the past. A generally revitalising and energising stone, it can help to banish lethargy, apathy and exhaustion. Mentally, peridot motivates growth and enhances transformation through making necessary changes in your life.

Overall, this delightful green gem promotes psychological wellbeing, clarity and ultimately, spiritual truth. It accelerates personal growth and enhances a feeling of inner joy and lightness, opening you up to giving, receiving and expressing their associated emotions.

Peridot is a visionary crystal, which helps you to discover your destiny and your spiritual purpose, making it an excellent working stone for healers and diviners alike.

★ PHENACITE ★

Astrological Affinities ★ Sagittarius, Pisces

Magical Tips ★ It is highly recommended that this stone be used in combination with yellow sapphire and/or cinnabar quartz to attract financial abundance and prosperity.

Vibration ★ Earthy to High

Phenacite is a rare mineral which often crystallises in short prisms. A great Third Eye awakener, phenacite is a supreme stone of spirituality, its pulsing energies felt at the Third Eye even by people not normally sensitive to crystal energies. This stimulation is stronger than one can receive from virtually any other stone. It can also be used to awaken the latent special capacities residing in the prefrontal lobes, the newest and most advanced region of the human brain, sometimes bringing spontaneous experiences of telepathy, psychokinesis, prophetic visions, or remote viewing (intuitively sensing faraway situations).

Phenacite's link with the higher realms make it a powerful tool for the manifestation of inner images or patterns of intention in the outer physical world.

★ PREHNITE ★

Astrological Affinities ★ Cancer, Pisces

Magical Tips ★ Prehnite can enable one to trust in the Universe again and restore the soul's belief in Divine manifestation.

The serene prehnite is a stone of unconditional love. Prehnite has an ethereal quality to it when tumbled, cut and polished, and often has a pearly lustre. Though not always easy to find, it is well worth searching for. This is an ideal stone to 'heal the healer' and when meditating with this stone, you are put in touch with the Universe's energy grid.

The Higher Self may be contacted through this gem, and it is said to help one connect with angels and other spiritual and extra-terrestrial realms.

Prehnite enhances inner knowing, precognition and attuning to Divine energies. It can bring about prophecy and light the way forward for your spiritual growth.

Prehnite is a protective stone, sealing the aura in a shield of loving energy, calming the environment and surrounding you with peace, security, and protection. It aligns with the Solar Plexus and Heart chakras, enhancing and balancing the flow of energy along all the chakra points.

Overall, prehnite is an excellent stone to use for relaxation, clarity of thought, and soulful bonding within personal relationships.

★ PYRITE ★

Astrological Affinities ★ Aries, Leo, Fire Element

Magical Tips ★ To best ensure the success of pyrite's positive properties, position them where they can soak up the powerful and energising light of the Sun. According to feng shui, pyrite is one of the best stones to attract the energy of wealth and abundance. It can be used as a cluster, sphere or cube, as well as in combination with a variety of other popular 'cures' for finances, such as Chinese coins, lucky Buddhas, et cetera. If you are using pyrite as a feng shui money-attractor, the best spot to place it in is the Wealth & Prosperity corner of your home (furthest left corner of your dwelling, as seen from the entrance, at 11 o'clock).

Pyrite, or iron pyrite, is an earthy metallic crystal associated with the Earth element, to help bring forth its riches and to promote the fertility and good fortune of a project or to boost your own financial investments. Also known as fool's gold, Inca stone and fire stone *, pyrite often appears as a beautiful golden mineral that has fooled many a prospector in their quest for the real thing. Pyrite has its place in modern day science and alchemy also, being used as a good source of sulphuric acid by scientists and alchemists for the last 1,000 years. Pyrite is essentially a brassy, silver to gold-coloured iron mineral which occurs in clusters, chunks, cubes, and more rarely as flat, circular plates often called 'Suns' or 'sand dollars'.

Lapis lazuli, an enchanting deep blue stone with gold 'flecks', contains pyrite, as do other crystals such as praziolite and schorl.

A piece of pyrite placed on a desk energises the area around it. It is helpful when planning large business concepts, by helping one tap into one's ability and potential and stimulating the flow of ideas. It is also believed to attract prosperity.

Pyrite works well with all the chakras and makes a good companion for amethyst in the development of spiritual vision and psychic abilities. Used upon the Third Eye, it will assist in its development. As a stone that enhances concentration and memory, pyrite will help ground any spiritual or psychic insights amethyst gives rise to, and imprint these understandings upon your cellular memory. Mental activity is accelerated by pyrite as physically it can increase blood flow to the brain. Associated with the blood, eyes and brain, it can promote cleansing and healing of all these areas.

Pyrite resonates with the energies of the Sun and is joyous and uplifting. It can be used on the Solar Plexus chakra for the purpose of enhancing personal and psychic power and to transmit thought-forms to another or the Universe. It can also be used at the Base and Crown chakras simultaneously to open the chakras and to ground the information received.

Pyrite also possesses protective qualities, shielding against negative influences and discordant energies, sending them back to their source.

Psychologically, pyrite relieves anxiety, melancholy, deep despair and frustration, and boosts self-worth and confidence.

* Pyrite is also known as fire stone, because it gives off sparks when struck with a hard object. This makes it a potential fire hazard in mines. For this reason, combined with its often mistaken identity for real gold, pyrite is disliked by miners.

★ QUARTZ ~ CINNABAR QUARTZ * ★

Main Spiritual & Metaphysical Qualities ★ Releases energy blockages; realigns the chakras; attracts abundance & magic; increases strength & vigour; enables the soul to raise its vibration to the highest frequency, to allow harnessing the power of the gods.

Astrological Affinities ★ Aries, Gemini, Virgo, Scorpio, Mercury

Magical Tips ★ As a stone of the Magician archetype, cinnabar (or cinnabar quartz) can facilitate the alignment of personal will with Divine will, allowing one to 'tweak' the Divine currents so that one can influence creative material manifestation. Place cinnabar stones at your Base and Crown chakras to activate and stimulate spiritual alchemy at your centre. Cinnabar, along with other abundance-attracting crystals such as topaz, sunstone, carnelian, jade and turquoise, has thousands of years of historical use as charms and amulets to support its manifesting powers. Cinnabar jewellery carved with prosperity symbols was popular in ancient Asia, and it is a well-known tool in the art of Feng Shui, being used in ornaments and jewellery that are known to attract great wealth. Overall, you can use cinnabar to attract more money into your life.

Vibration ★ Earthy

Mercury's ore is cinnabar, believed to be one of the most powerful stones on the planet for abundance. Alchemy, magic, transformation, wealth, insight, manifestation and mental agility are all key words for the mixture of red cinnabar, white quartz and other trace minerals that comprise what is known as cinnabar quartz. Its element is Fire and it is connected with the Base, Sacral and Third Eye chakras.

A very attractive stone, cinnabar's colour is usually vermilion or scarlet red. It forms around volcanic vents and hot springs and may also occur in sedimentary rocks associated with recent volcanic activity; cinnabar is often found in veins cooling near these volcanic disturbances. Cinnabar becomes cinnabar quartz when it forms in conjunction with quartz, and cinnabar quartz is the most potent form of this crystal for metaphysical use. The quartz serves to increase the durability of the stone, as well as magnifying cinnabar's energetic properties.

Cinnabar on its own attracts abundance and increases the powers of persuasion, as well as assisting organisation, business and finance. It imparts fluency of the mind and speech, releases energy blockages and aligns energy centres. Cinnabar is also aligned with the god Mercury, also known as Hermes or Thoth, and as such it can help increase mental agility, intellectual brilliance and clarity of thought, traits for which these gods were known.

The usual colour of cinnabar, pure red, is resonant with the colour of one of the images of the Philosopher's Stone, the 'attainment' of which is the goal of alchemy. This is the Stone of the 'lovers of wisdom' (*philo* = love; *sopher* = wisdom, or Sophia), which helps the alchemists attain one of their loftiest aims aside from transmuting lead to gold - that of wisdom or enlightenment. For one's aspirations of spiritual growth and evolution, Cinnabar is a powerful quickener, helping to speed up the process by which one's transformation can occur.

Overall, this mysterious and captivating stone facilitates the process of alchemical change within the individual and brings about the experience and illuminated expression of one's newfound inner golden-hued awareness.

* Cinnabar and Cinnabar Quartz contain mercury, so caution should be exercised when handling this crystal. Wash hands thoroughly after use.

★ QUARTZ ~ HERKIMER DIAMOND ★

Main Spiritual & Metaphysical Qualities ★ Soul retrieval; integrates body, mind, soul & spirit into a harmonious whole; powerful agent of transmutation & purification; restores equilibrium; accelerates spiritual growth.

Astrological Affinities ★ Scorpio

Magical Tips ★ If you are feeling overwrought about a particular problem or circumstance, place one under your pillow so that the energy of the stone will encourage you to remember your dreams and therefore help provide some insights into how you can resolve a troubling issue. Herkimer diamond also attunes you to the highest source of soul guidance, by connecting you to the All That Is to manifest your spiritual potential on Earth.

Vibration ★ Exceptionally High

Herkimer quartz 'diamonds' are a special variety of quartz crystal found in and around Herkimer, New York (U.S.). Herkimer diamonds are so named because their small, short, stubby, double-terminated shapes and lustrous surfaces make them resemble real diamonds somewhat; however they are not real diamonds. Also known as the dream crystal, Herkimer diamonds are excellent for helping you to feel balanced and alert. With a hardness of around 7.5, they are harder than most other quartz varieties, which may be because they are formed in a hard-rock matrix.

Keywords for this attractive glossy stone are purification, visions, dreams, spiritualisation of physical life, and vibrational ascension. This clear-coloured crystal works with the complementary energies of yin (feminine, passive energy) and yang (masculine active energy) to help attune you spiritually, and aids in bringing in teachings from a dream or trance state.

Herkimers can inspire powerful soul-healing and can energise water by imbuing it with their powerful properties, thereby creating a potent healing elixir.

Herkimer diamond enhances visualisation, astral travel, and dream recall, as well as helping to amplify and 'store' thoughts. They are most effective when used on the Crown chakra, as they are manifestations of pure, solidified spiritual light. Herkimers emanate a strong, harmonious energy that positively dwells on the upper levels of the quartz vibrational spectrum; they can also pick up and magnify the frequencies of other stones.

★ QUARTZ ~ ROSE QUARTZ ★

The Love Stone

Main Spiritual & Metaphysical Qualities ★ Promotes love & friendship; strengthens Heart chakra; aids forgiveness; promotes feelings of love; enhances self-love; alleviates depression; aids relaxation & meditation; balances the emotions; encourages reconciliation; dissolves guilt & bitterness; encourages forgiveness; eases trauma associated with abuse of all kinds.

Astrological Affinities ★ Taurus, Libra, Pisces, Venus

Magical Tips ★ Rose quartz is, quite simply, the stone of pure love which encourages you to live from your heart! This beautiful pale pink stone is attuned all kinds of love and helps to activate and open you up to romantic blessings and encounters. Gently empowering, on a metaphysical level, rose quartz can open up and balance the Heart chakra to attract love of all kinds into your life. All you need to do is choose which kind of love you desire, infuse your crystal with this intention, wear it from thereon, and it will do the work for you if you believe it will, all the while keeping your heart and mind open to opportunities as they arise.

Vibration ★ Earthy & High

This soft pink translucent stone is quite simply and universally known as the 'Stone of Love'. Unobtrusive though it is, this unassuming yet alluring crystal should never be underrated. The minuscule crystals of which it is composed give it amazing durability, and the addition of titanium, a metallic element of profound strength, not only accounts for its agreeable colouring but gives it the power to work wonders on physical and emotional pains and scars. Calming to the spirit and banishing fear and violent tendencies, aggressive energies find it difficult to survive in its presence.

Balancing and calming, rose quartz has been used for centuries to heal the heart, attract love, ease emotional pain, foster self-acceptance, treat fertility problems, and overcome traumas. It also helps one to develop a spirit of forgiveness and trust.

Rose quartz is connected with the Heart chakra and is known as the stone of unconditional love, enhancing all forms of this omnipresent force and opening up the heart to give and receive these energies.

Its pink colour associated with Venus, the planet of love and desire, rose quartz is tender and passionate, comforting and sensual, erotic and nurturing, and affectionate and amorous, all at the same time. Like its ruler Venus, this crystal's energies also promote receptivity to beauty of all kinds.

Reassuring and soft, rose quartz helps to strengthen your empathy and sensitivity. If you have never received love, it will fill your heart; if you have loved and lost, it comforts your grief.

Rose quartz is a gentle stone, helping to balance all of the bodily systems and restore a sense of peace and tranquillity; it is an excellent gem to use for bringing harmony to a chaotic situation. It can also be placed under the pillow to encourage more restful sleep and to ease insomnia. Useful during stressful, dramatic or traumatic situations, rose quartz can empower you to feel more positive, potent, loving and accepting. Holding, wearing or carrying it also enhances positive affirmations, and helps you to foster self-worth and acceptance.

The energies this soothing stone radiates can and should be shared, by giving rose quartz to those in need of comfort a boost of self-confidence and reassurance.

As pure and virtuous as this crystal is however, because it tends to absorb negative energies, it should be cleansed regularly if used for healing purposes. It can be cleaned under fresh, running water, then left out in the Sun for a short period to dry, restore, and re-charge.

Overall, rose quartz has the power to instil a sense of infinite peace in your heart. Releasing emotional wounds, encouraging forgiveness and compassion for the Self and others, and assisting with all love matters, it heals and opens your heart on every level, imparting the gentle wisdom and Truth that *love is all there is.*

★ QUARTZ ~ RUTILE QUARTZ ★

Astrological Affinities ★ Gemini, Virgo

Magical Tips ★ If you need an extra charge of energy, the rutile - or rutilated - quartz is a good crystal to use or wear; it contains tiny needles that act as rapid conductors of energy. Also, each piece of rutilated quartz is thought to contain a guardian spirit who will protect the owner or user from harm. Rutilated quartz is a powerful healer which enhances the life force, encourages inspiration and will uplift the healing energies of all other stones. On a mystical level, its aids scrying, channelling and astral travel.

Vibration ★ Earthy & High

Properly named rutilated quartz and also known as 'angel hair' and 'Venus's hair', this stone is actually clear quartz rock crystal with fine, hair-like 'needles' of golden and reddish hue. Its appearance is that of long thick 'threads' in clear crystal. These strands comprise the reddish-brown mineral known as rutile, which carries an ethereal vibration that enhances attunement to the Divine and higher Self. Rutile intensifies the healing power of quartz, thus making this an ideal stone for the magnification of goals. Due to the age of the rutile, it is associated with past lives and alternate realities.

Rutile quartz is an effective integrator of energy at any and all levels, heightening the energetic impulse of quartz. Indeed, it is a very efficient vibrational healer. Rutile quartz is said to have the perfect balance of cosmic light and to be an illuminator for the soul, promoting spiritual growth as well as cleansing and energising the aura. Psychologically, rutilated quartz reaches the root of problems and facilitates changes of direction and transitions.

Protective against psychic attack, rutile quartz is useful in supporting one's energy field during emotional release or confrontation with the darker aspects of the psyche. It also connects one to soul lessons, soul plans, and one's present life purpose.

Excellent for alleviating exhaustion and energy depletion, this powerful variety of quartz can ease dark moods and depression, and soothe anxiety, stress, fears, phobias and self-loathing. Venus's hair can be used to encourage your belief in yourself if you are feeling negative or self-critical; it can de-clutter your mind and change your mental outlook to a more cheerful, hopeful one. It is also helpful for therapists as it filters negative energies from clients, while at the same time supporting their energy field; it supports and protects healers' auric space, and guards against 'attack' from the shadowy aspects of the psyche.

Overall, Venus's hair facilitates contact with the highest spiritual guidance and breaks down those barriers which are hindering one's personal progress and evolution. An efficient all-round healer, this stone draws away negative energy and breaks down the barriers which may be blocking spiritual progress. It also assists in allowing one to let go of the past.

Spiritually, this crystal is said to have a perfect balance of cosmic light and to be an illuminator for the soul, promoting spiritual growth; further, it aids astral travel, channelling and scrying, and facilitates contact with your highest spiritual guidance.

Rutile quartz promotes forgiveness on all levels and opens the aura to allow healing. It heals the soul and facilitates the regeneration and reformation of damaged soul fragments. Wearing rutilated quartz will help to integrate all parts of your being into a balanced, holistic whole.

Wherever you are on the Path, carrying or wearing rutilated quartz, or Venus's hair as it is more mystically known, will empower you for the journey.

★ QUARTZ ~ SMOKY QUARTZ ★

Main Spiritual & Metaphysical Qualities ★ Grounding; transmutes negative energies; restores vigour & strength; shines a light on the shadows of your inner being; cleanses all chakras & shields the aura.

Astrological Affinities ★ Sagittarius, Capricorn, Pisces, Earth Element

Magical Tips ★ Smoky quartz was an essential ingredient in ancient magicians' tool kits. Smoky quartz plays a unique role in the area of manifestation and can be used to attract to you what you need in order to manifest. Because of the specific colour and trace elements in this form of quartz, it responds to your intent of radiating to attract to you the right things you need for your aspect of manifestation. This can be done by setting up one smoky quartz near where you sleep and asking it to help you in attracting the right situations and conditions you need. Charge a smoky quartz when performing magic or making a wish on a New Moon, then observe as your work rapidly comes into being before the Moon becomes full again.

Vibration ★ Earthy & High

Smoky quartz is the darker coloured quartz with a smoky-grey-coloured appearance. This is a manifestation stone and helps seeded projects come into fruition. You can consciously place your intent into the crystal to bring to you the right people or circumstances to make your desire a reality. The power of prayer or affirmation works to reinforce the reality of the good of all involved, including yourself.

Smoky quartz, like amethyst, is also protective and has the ability to protect your energy field from unhelpful forces. It promotes stability, pride and joy, improves intuition, provides clarity of thought and, resonating with the Base chakra, enhances our survival and security instincts.

An excellent grounding, centering and protective stone which dispels negativity and allows us to tap into our subconscious wisdom, smoky quartz helps make our wishes, desires and dreams come true by grounding their essence in reality.

A charming stone that often contains rainbow inclusions, smoky quartz is a special gem that brings abundance, good fortune and prosperity.

★ QUARTZ ~ TIBETAN QUARTZ ★

Astrological Affinities ★ All zodiac signs

Tibetan 'black' quartz is a purifying stone with the vibration of 'OM'. Found in the Himalayan Mountains of Tibet and Nepal, this stone offers the powers of spiritual protection and purification, enhancement of meditation, clearing and energising the aura, and the purification of desire.

Tibetan quartz is an intense stone which, when used on the Third Eye, can aid deep inner journeying. Regarded as being amongst the most powerful gems of spiritual protection ever found, this gemstone will purify an area and cleanse it of any negative influences.

Tibetan quartz emanates energies which can activate, harmonise and balance all chakras and meridian systems. Wearing or carrying this stone will help cleanse one's aura and form a protective field around it to guard against surrounding discordant energies, as well as assisting to ground the wearer and dissolve energy blockages.

A potent and sacred stone of the Light, Tibetan quartz is highly sought after for its metaphysical, healing, spiritual and balancing properties.

★ RHODOCHROSITE ★

Main Spiritual & Metaphysical Qualities ★ Allows you to recognise the Divine within yourself; promotes unconditional love & compassion; encourages self-love; profoundly healing.

Astrological Affinities ★ Aries, Leo, Scorpio, Sagittarius

Magical Tips ★ You can program rhodochrosite to attract a soul mate or 'twin flame', someone with whom you can connect and share unconditional love. It is also effective in opening up the Heart chakra to receive Divine love.

Vibration ★ Earthy to High

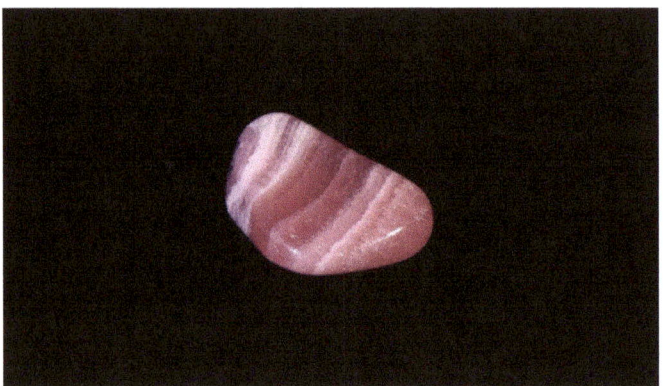

Otherwise known as 'Inca Rose' due to the belief it contained the blood of that civilisation's ancestral rulers, rhodochrosite was only discovered about sixty years ago, so like its cousin rhodonite, is new in holistic terms.

Rhodochrosite is found in two varieties: the sunset-coloured stone of gem quality, and the white-lined, rosy or baby-pink semi-precious gemstone. Tests have shown that both have beneficial properties, emitting light vibrations which cheer the depressed, preserve youth, and help to coax back the life-force into sickly subjects.

On a spiritual level, rhodochrosite represents selfless love and compassion. It expands the consciousness and integrates the spiritual with the material. Encouraging a dynamic and positive attitude, rhodochrosite is an excellent stone for the heart and relationships, particularly for people who feel unloved or unlovable. It is a stone which improves self-worth, lifts despondency, and soothes emotional stress. Mentally enlivening, it promotes the spontaneous expression of feelings, including passionate and erotic urges. Because it prompts spontaneity, it is ideal for those who find it difficult to express their emotions.

Rhodochrosite also enhances dream states, creativity and lightness of being and feeling. Although rhodochrosite has a charming reputation for having the ability to attract one's soul mate, this may not be the blissful experience hoped for, as a soul mate may be someone who appears in our life to teach us important, though not always pleasant, lessons for our higher good. In general terms however, it is a beautiful stone for drawing love into your experience in whatever form it takes.

Rhodochrosite works on the Solar Plexus, Base and Heart chakras, gently bringing painful and repressed feelings to the surface, allowing them to be acknowledged in order to then be dissipated and released. It is even believed to be an effective stone for helping to heal the effects of sexual abuse. As a stone which resonates with the heart, it encourages staying open and teaches the heart to assimilate hurtful feelings without shutting down. It is a stone which removes denial and insists that you face the truth about yourselves and others with loving awareness instead of evasion.

Rhodochrosite is a perfect companion for rose quartz when working on the Heart chakra. It is an emotional balancer, trauma-soother and resonates with the subtle bodies, swiftly clearing the Sacral, Solar Plexus and Heart chakras of traumatic events and feelings. In fact, it unblocks all psychic chakra energy centres so light and power can flow upwards into the body from the Earth via the Base chakra, from the natural world through the Heart chakra, and helps draw cosmic energy from above through the Crown chakra; all this will enable you to move towards the future after periods of doubt, and express love without fear of rejection.

Overall, rhodochrosite holds the higher octave of love that can dissolve emotional wounds and is a powerful psychological tonic and heart-healer.

★ RHODONITE ★

Main Spiritual & Metaphysical Qualities ★ Instils emotional balance; aids self-confidence & self-esteem; increases energy levels; deepens the ties of friendship; gives clarity of ideas; heals heart wounds; helps you to stay heart-centred; relieves a traumatic past; promotes reflection; alleviates confusion, shock & stress; encourages unconditional love & acceptance; instils a sense of self-trust.

Astrological Affinities ★ Taurus, Cancer

Vibration ★ Earthy

Rhodonite is a more recently discovered crystal, first found in 1819 and so has no special folklore associated with it. It is a striking pink-violet stone with black colouring that takes its name from the Greek word 'rhodos' meaning 'rose' or 'rose-coloured'.

Often found near silver mines, rhodonite can vary from delicate pink to light, rosy red, with its trademark black or gold veins running throughout its structure. As a pink stone, it naturally works well with the Heart chakra and has a positive effect on general health and wellbeing. Because rhodonite is associated with love and friendship, it can be used to attract love into your life, but not before first working on your own self-acceptance and self-love; indeed, rhodonite works on the principle that when you accept yourself, the resulting energy will attract the love you desire.

An emotional balancer that nurtures compassion and encourages the brotherhood of humanity, rhodonite stimulates, clears and activates the Heart chakra. It encourages us to forgive and forget past traumas, allowing the heart to heal, and enables us to express the purity of unconditional love towards both ourselves and others. It also helps build confidence and self-esteem.

Rhodonite also grounds energy and helps one to achieve their potential. Psychologically it helps to heal and dispel negative emotions, anxiety, fear and panic attacks. It should be used as soon as possible after a traumatic event to restore balance, calmness and harmony to the wearer. In fact, it can be used as a gem essence to help alleviate shock or trauma (but should never replace appropriate and qualified medical assistance).

Rhodonite has beneficial effects on the nervous system, so where feelings such as jealousy, anger, bitterness, irritability, selfishness and depression have been suppressed, rhodonite allows them to rise to the surface to be healed and released.

★ RUBY ★

Stone of the Sun

> *The most precious of gems, a balm in the hour of trial, grief, bereavement, disappointment, a soother of agitation and disburdener of the oppressed soul.*

Charubel

Main Spiritual & Metaphysical Qualities ★ Enhances passion in life & love; promotes positive self-esteem, transmutes anger & other negative feelings into positive energy; imparts a vital & dynamic outlook; alleviates apathy; creates a courageous & potent frame of mind; calms hyperactivity; instils inner peace & tranquillity; alleviates insomnia.

Astrological Affinities ★ The Sun, Aries, Cancer, Leo, Scorpio, Sagittarius, Capricorn, Mars, Fire Element

Magical Tips ★ Ruby is a stone of immense power and vitality and can be worn to stimulate pure life force energy. Its spirit is a great ally to those who wish to work magic in their lives. Ruby is one of the stones of abundance and aids in retaining wealth and a healthy, driven passion. Astarte, the Mesopotamian goddess of war, fertility and motherhood, was said to own a ruby that illuminated her temple with a supernatural glow.

Ruby derives its name from the Latin *rubens* or *rubeus*, meaning 'red'. A variety of the mineral corundum, it is a very hard stone, having a hardness of 9 on the Mohs scale. The ancients considered ruby to be the stone of the Sun and believed it represented Fire and the life force. Because it symbolised happiness and brightness and was believed to be the most beautiful and striking of gems, it came to be associated with the sign of Leo. This association was also made because of its reputation for drawing success, wealth and joy, its symbolic virtues including courage, nobility, spirit and loyalty. Ruby has long been regarded as a symbol of love, beauty, passion, success, strength, protection and power.

Ruby is one of the four precious gemstones (the others being diamond, sapphire and emerald), worn since ancient times to signify high status. It is most commonly associated with love, especially faithful, passionate commitment, and helps older women to value their beauty and the wisdom of their life experience.

Rubies are said to bring prophetic dreams and banish nightmares; to dream of them is a sign of coming prosperity and good fortune.

The gem of northern summer, ruby burns with a captivating fire. It aids in strengthening and refining the natural abilities you were born with. Imparting vigour to your journey, it energises and balances but may sometimes overstimulate more delicate or irritable types.

Ruby encourages the setting of realistic goals, improves motivation and stimulates passion for living. It stimulates the Heart chakra and enlivens the heart, encouraging you to 'follow your bliss'. It is also a powerful energiser for the Base chakra. As a vitaliser for this energy centre, ruby signifies and arouses lust, and is strongly linked to the sexual and reproductive organs. It can be used to release any energy blockages deep within the self, and to activate, vitalise, intensify and increase desire.

Ruby gets things moving; it utilises infrared, the slowest vibration of the colour spectrum, giving a new boost to situations or circumstances that have been sluggish or stagnant.

Carrying the positive and powerful red ray, ruby brings up anger and other negative energies, transmutes them, and removes anything unfavourable from your path. It can even shield you from outside forces that are draining to your energy.

Promoting lively leadership and confidence, ruby brings about a positive and courageous state of mind.

Essentially, ruby is a dynamic and captivating stone which charges up passion, banishes sadness, warns of danger or imminent misfortune (apparently by darkening in colour), fires up enthusiasm, increases one's sex drive and vitality, and helps to overcome exhaustion, apathy and lethargy by imparting potency and vigour.

Emitting an abundance of cheerfulness, ruby renews one's passion for life, and instils a sense of Truth, courage, wisdom and perseverance.

★ SAPPHIRE ★

The Wisdom Stone

Main Spiritual & Metaphysical Qualities ★ Prophecy; ascension; mastery; stimulates imagination & curiosity; highlights the truth; enhances meditation; brings inner peace, serenity & wisdom; strengthens the virtue of sincerity; helps us to prevail in love & friendships; promotes love, sincerity & generous commitment.

Astrological Affinities ★ Aries, Taurus, Libra, Virgo, Jupiter, Saturn, Air Element

Magical Tips ★ Sapphire is one of the great metaphysical healing gems of Vedic astrology. Especially prized by the ancient Greeks and appearing throughout their mythology, those who wished to put a question to the famous Delphic Oracle had to wear a sapphire. Labelled the 'Gem of the Heavens', sapphire was believed to bestow its wearer with strengthened vision, including prophetic visions of the future. Some sapphires are believed to be record-keepers and may aid you to access the knowledge of ancient civilisations when dreaming, 'journeying' or meditating. Use it to connect to your spirit guides and teachers and for interdimensional communication, as it connects mind, body and spirit.

Vibration ★ High

The hardest crystal after diamond, sapphire has long held a reputation for its amazing spiritual as well as physical properties. A variety of the mineral corundum, sapphire is a symbol of ultimate truth and imminent justice. Sapphire is found in a variety of colours, including blue, yellow, white, black, purple and green - but the blue variety is probably the best known.

Known as the wisdom stone, each colour carrying its own particular 'knowledge', all hues bring prosperity and attract gifts of many kinds. Sapphire has always been associated with love, fidelity, joy, prosperity, the heavens and the angels. It is a potent symbol of truth and constancy.

Sapphire's name is derived from the Sanskrit word *Sani*, which means Saturn. Yellow sapphire is aligned with the planet Jupiter, the planet of spiritual ascension and mastery. In Vedic astrology, gemstones such as the blue and yellow sapphires are believed to work through physiochemical and electrochemical means.

Sapphire was believed to encourage altruism and generosity, to stimulate the imagination and curiosity, and had the reputation of winning those who wore it numerous friendships.

There are many legends surrounding this luminous blue stone: the Ten Commandments were said to be written on tablets of sapphire, and King Solomon was believed to have used one to commune with God. An old Persian myth tells that the Earth sat on a giant sapphire which gave the sky its brilliant blue colour. In Buddhism, sapphire is known as the 'stone of the stones' because of its connection with the virtuous qualities of devotion, happiness, tranquillity, and spiritual enlightenment.

Due to its highly soothing and balancing effect, sapphire is beneficial for treating nervous conditions such as panic attacks, anxiety and stress.

Sapphires (especially star sapphires *) are good stones to work with to improve your psychic faculties or astral travel, stimulating the Third Eye chakra to enhance psychic experiences. Sapphire is also effective at activating and stimulating the Crown Chakra, and is excellent for improving mental focus and clarity.

Blue sapphire has a calming and balancing effect on emotions and may also be used to open up the Crown and Third Eye chakras to the angelic realms. Being a blue-hued gem, sapphire resonates strongly with the Throat chakra, promoting truth, communication and self-expression.

Overall, blue sapphire encourages you to reach for the stars, speak your truth, and stay on your rightful spiritual path.

Star Sapphire ★ The six-rayed star seen in certain sapphires, known as star sapphire, is caused by the presence of a radiating pattern of needle-like formations within the stone.

Yellow Sapphire, The Stone of Jupiter ★ Yellow Sapphire is Jupiter's stone and known in crystal circles as a stone of abundance that attracts wealth. Jupiter is an optimistic and benevolent planet. It represents good fortune and governs philosophy, religion, spirituality, wisdom, success, expansion, and prosperity. Yellow sapphire also has astrological affinities with Leo, Sagittarius, Pisces, and the Air Element. This enchanting yellow stone is a type of conundrum, usually a blue gem, coloured by iron and titanium. It can have tones of gold or orange, but the best gems for Jupiter are lemon-yellow. Vedic tradition recommends that the yellow sapphire should be transparent, of a uniform colour, sparkling, and smooth with a soft lustre. Worn at propitious moments, this jewel is said to bring luck, peace and prosperity, and to impart vitality, wisdom and longevity.

★ SELENITE ★

Main Spiritual & Metaphysical Qualities ★ Connects you to All That Is; illuminates your inner temple; helps one to access angelic realms; encourages connection to the Wise Feminine Divine powers; quietens mental chatter; emotionally stabilising; auric cleanser & healer.

Astrological Affinities ★ Cancer, Scorpio, Pisces, Water Element

Magical Tips ★ Selenite stands at the threshold between matter and spirit, and as such it rapidly opens and activates the Third Eye, Crown and Soul Star (above the head) chakras. In fact, its intensity is quite remarkable, and a wand made from this crystal pointed at the Third Eye sends energy that can feel like a gust of wind going through the forehead and out the top of the head; attaching other stones to a selenite wand can also magnify those stones' energies. An eleventh century lapidary states that selenite actually 'grows' with the waxing Moon and diminishes as the Moon wanes.

Vibration ★ Exceptionally High

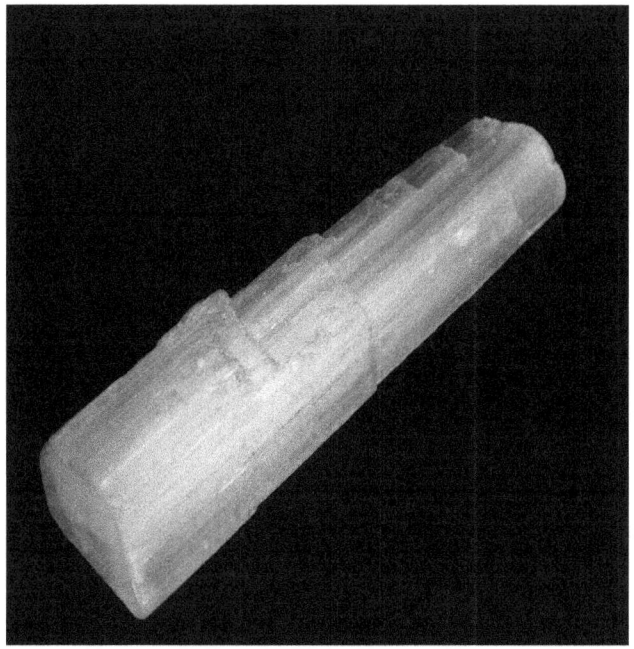

Selenite is a form of gypsum that is called selenite if it is relatively clear and well-formed. It has a hardness of 2, and some selenite crystals have the startling property of being soft and flexible enough to be bent in one's hands. This crystal can be colourless (similar to clear quartz in appearance), white, green, grey or golden-brown, and is found in many countries including Australia, Greece, and the Americas. The ones from Mexico are the most popular ones for metaphysical use, being used to make spheres, lamps, wands and a variety of other spiritual tools and talismans.

Selenite's key themes are spiritual activation, communion with the 'higher self', attuning one to the Universal mind, and the integration of heart awareness with the mind. Enhancing mental clarity and concentration, it has a positive effect on the brain.

Selenite, or gypsum as it is often referred to, is one of the most powerful stones of the New Age. It brings light into the energetic bodies and instantly clears all the chakras. It is one of the few stones that does not ever need to be cleansed and can be used to cleanse other stones was well.

Selenite wands are very powerful healing tools, being used to direct energy and acting as an extension of your energy and intent. Fast and effective at cleansing one's auric field, it can raise one's awareness to higher planes of inner experience as well, making it possible to meet one's spirit guides and guardian angels.

Selenite, especially the clear variety that naturally occurs in wand or rod form, is deeply linked with the Water element; in fact, Water occurs in the interior of many of these wands, and water is key in the growth of selenite. The huge selenite crystals from Chihuahua, Mexico, were formed in a water-saturated cave.

In meditation, selenite soothes the nerves, enhances willpower, and stimulates the flow of spiritual energies throughout one's physical body, as well as the astral and etheric bodies. Selenite, when used in meditation, can assist in facilitating the integration of the left and right sides of the brain. The great 'myth' of the human condition portrays these two brains as if they were separate beings - the rational/materialist left and the idealist/creative right. The resolution of their seemingly insoluble conflict can instigate great healing.

Note ★ Selenite dissolves in water and should not be cleansed using this method. Instead, it can be re-energised by placing it on a bed of brown rice under the Moon's rays.

★ SHATTUCKITE ★

The Wish Granter

Astrological Affinities ★ Taurus, Libra, Aquarius, Venus

Magical Tips ★ Shattukite is said to link one with the Gateway to the healing light. It is also believed to grant wishes, by connecting one with one's True Path, which then place you in direct contact with the serendipities, coincidences and synchronicities that enable you to fulfil your deepest desires.

Shattukite is an unusual and visually striking mineral composed of blue copper that may also contain traces of dioptase, chrysocolla, malachite or smoky quartz. It is useful in healing past life grief, repressed trauma, and other emotional manifestations that are trapped in the human auric field.

Psychically, this enchanting gemstone can open up psychic channels to facilitate mediumship, channelling ability, intuition, and automatic writing.

Because Shattukite connects one with the Divine, it has the mystical ability to place you in exactly the right places for the unfoldment of your highest personal evolution and potentials.

★ SPINEL ★

Astrological Affinities ★ Aries, Taurus, Gemini, Cancer, Leo, Virgo, Libra, Scorpio, Sagittarius, Fire Element

Spinel is a chameleon among jewels, occurring in a wider range of tints than any other variety of stone. It is rarer than ruby or sapphire, with which it is often found, and it has a similar hardness to these two, a considerable 7.5 to 8 (the ancients classified the red spinel as a 'female ruby').

Spinel is a beautiful crystal, coming in colours of white, red, violet, black, green, blue, brown, orange, yellow and colourless. Connected with energy renewal, it opens the chakras and facilitates movement of kundalini energy up the spine, offering encouragement in challenging circumstances.

Spinel has rejuvenating and restorative properties and enhances the positive aspects of one's character. Colourless, or clear, spinel stimulates mysticism and communication with higher realms. It links the chakras of the physical body with the Crown chakra of the etheric body, facilitating enlightenment and visionary experiences.

Blue spinel stimulates and facilitates communication and channelling and is aligned with the Throat chakra.

Green spinel stimulates love, kindness and compassion, and opens the Heart chakra.

Overall, spinel is a hardwearing stone and occurs in the same crystal systems as the diamond. The planets Uranus and Venus are co-rulers of this stone, with the result that spinel, on the spiritual plane, is effectively directed towards promoting general idealism through harmony, originality, creativity, and uniquely, in the making of beautiful music.

★ STAUROLITE ★

Astrological Affinities ★ Gemini, Libra, Aquarius, Air Element

Magical Tips ★ The cross formation signifies the meeting of spirit and matter, death and rebirth, and so it is with our leaving behind our past as we move onto our higher spiritual destiny. Staurolite shows that the transition from darkness into light is easier than we think.

Staurolite is usually a vibrant red or grey-brown stone, which derives its name from the Greek word *staurus*, meaning 'cross', as it is naturally cruciform. The Ancient Britons called these gems 'fairy stones' and used them in magical rites. They are called fairy stones because according to tradition, they are the tears shed by fairies upon hearing of Jesus' suffering on the cross. The early Christians knew them as 'cross stones' and wore them as lucky charms, while myths speak of 'staurolite stars' falling from heaven. President Teddy Roosevelt is said to have carried one of these natural crosses mounted on his watch as a good luck charm.

Staurolite today is known as the Fairy Cross and is traditionally a protective stone used as an amulet for good luck. This stone is said to connect the physical, etheric and spiritual planes, promoting communication between them.

Known as a Gemini power crystal, it is exceptionally useful at relieving nervous tension due to overwork or simply having too many things on the boil, as Airy folk are prone to do. Physically, staurolite provides a grounding energy for Airy souls also, and is especially useful for those wishing to give up smoking; as well as healing its ill-effects, it can assist in understanding the hidden reasons behind the nicotine addiction and will help heal the break between our past and future lifestyles - at those points where our spiritual life must meet with our material existence, staurolite smoothes over the cracks and aligns all levels of our being so we can feel more comfortable with any changes. Encouraging a less materially-based existence, staurolite helps manifest only that which is needed to make our physical lives comfortable, and gently rejects that which does not benefit us spiritually.

★ STIBNITE ★

Main Spiritual & Metaphysical Qualities ★ Protective when journeying out of body; releases cords, ties & old belief patterns that are holding you down or back; soul retrieval; karmic healing; transformative.

Astrological Affinities ★ Scorpio, Capricorn

Magical Tips ★ In magical use, stibnite is regarded as a shaman's stone: facilitating shape-shifting and creating a powerful shield around the body while it is astrally or spiritually journeying. Hold stibnite to call your power animals. When used as a wand, stibnite separates the pure from the dross and reveals the inner gold in your centre.

Vibration ★ Earthy

Stibnite is expressed in straight radiating needles or flat rods, sometimes with criss-cross lines which are usually grouped in parallel.

It is an attractive stone occasionally exhibiting surface iridescence. Shamans used stibnite as a portal to pass between the upper and lower worlds where spirits, guides and power animals reside.

Stibnite has the power to break through illusions, enabling us to see the spiritual reality of All That Is. As such, it activates and opens the Third Eye and Crown charkas, draws out our inner power, and facilitates transformation.

Note ★ Stibnite can be toxic and should be handled with care. Hands should be washed thoroughly after use.

★ SUGILITE ★

Main Spiritual & Metaphysical Qualities ★ Aligns all chakras, working from Crown to Base; promotes inner peace; offers hope; helps you to live in the light of the truth; love; helps to heal shock & trauma; helps you move beyond disappointments; allows you to access & live through your heart's spiritual truths.

Astrological Affinities ★ Virgo, Sagittarius, Aquarius, Pisces

Magical Tips ★ Pink sugilite, especially in magenta or fuchsia shades, is a powerful love crystal; it can be worn in jewellery to attract a kindred spirit.

Vibration ★ Earthy & High

Pink sugilite comes in pink, magenta, fuchsia, and violet-purple hues, aligning it beautifully with the vibration of love. Pink sugilite is a stone of the heart and resolves inner hurts and disappointment. It helps maintain the balance between everyday practicalities and the spiritual world, and helps you rise above despair and despondency. This charming pink crystal also encourages a love of life and belief in the inherent goodness of others.

★ STAR DIOPSIDE ★

Astrological Affinities ★ Scorpio, Sagittarius, Aquarius, Pisces

Magical Tips ★ Star diopside provides a great deal of protection for those who are exploring deep spiritual paths, and will keep you connected to the Earth while journeying or travelling the Universe.

The resplendent star diopside can display a four-rayed hovering star with two sharp and two muted lines, hanging suspended over an almost opaque black-green to brownish-black body. Possibly the only top grade magnetic gemstone, star diopside contains needle-like crystals of magnetite that add to its beauty.

Star diopside is usually black, and when polished en cabochon, show's a cat's eye or star; it is therefore sometimes referred to as 'black star'. During the times of Atlantis and Lemuria, star diopside was used as a scrying stone, taking the seer into the depths. Indeed, it provides a link to otherworld energies and is excellent for exploring past life dimensions. An effective grounding stone for those undertaking astral travel, it can be used in combination with green barite for purging any unwanted entities you may encounter which are almost beings in themselves. Star diopside can act as a protective shield during these explorations and will absorb any excess forces that are cluttering the mind.

Psychologically, diopside assists you to remain detached and objective, stimulates the intellect, and helps to clear blocked emotions. When a decision needs to be made, consult a star diopside. Gaze into its shining surface and see the star within - which is actually *you* in your purest state.

★ SUNSTONE ★

The Abundance & Joy Stone

Main Spiritual & Metaphysical Qualities ★ Promotes achievement & success; alleviates depression & seasonal affective disorder (SAD); regenerative; vitalises the body, mind & spirit; removes negative conditioning & memories; instils a deep awareness of your own value; self-empowering; allows your true self to shine through.

Astrological Affinities ★ The Sun, Leo, Libra, Scorpio, Pisces

Magical Tips ★ Sunstone is an alchemical stone traditionally linked to the benevolent gods, good luck and fortune. It magnetises fame and good luck in competitions and can be worn to lead you to the resources to travel and for happy holidays or relocation to the Sun, and helps facilitate a profound connection to light and the regenerative powers of the Sun itself. Carry with Moonstone to integrate the god and goddess powers, animus and anima.

Vibration ★ Earthy

A joyful, light, uplifting and inspiring gem, sunstone is linked to the benevolent gods and instils good nature. This sparkling gem is associated with luck and good fortune, and acts as an anti-depressant, lifting dark moods. The two main types of sunstone are orange sunstone and yellow sunstone, sometimes known as golden labradorite. In some, a reddish iridescence, brought about by a minute inclusion of hematite and other minerals on a yellow or brownish-yellow background, is characteristic of this cheerful gem. The sunstone imitates the Sun by its red and gold spangled brilliance which glitters and gleams. Sunstone is formed within lava and, once it is released onto the Earth's surface, weathering of the lava reveals the crystals hidden within. It therefore attracts unexpected prosperity by uncovering your talents.

This stone represented the Sun god in ancient Greece and in some Native American rituals of the medicine wheel, it is placed in the centre and said to glow.

Yellow sunstone has an affinity for the Solar Plexus chakra and removes stress, anxiety and fear from this energy centre, suffusing it with light. An uplifting crystal, sunstone can fill you with love, laughter, confidence and inspiration. Its magical properties include magnetising abundance and all that you wish for, instilling an optimistic outlook, and even helping with bereavement and wistful reminiscing about the 'good old days' that can make one unable to enjoy the present. Overall, it is a joyful, light-inspiring stone that brings about *joie de vivre*. If life has lost is lustre, sunstone can help restore the shine, by clearing all the chakras and allowing the true self to shine through.

As a stone of good cheer, it can help dispel negative influences around you which are embedded in your aura or your chakras, removing the draining effects of other people, lovingly returning the contact to the other person through tie-cutting. It also assists with removing co-dependency tendencies, procrastination and depression, and facilitates independence, vitality and self-empowerment.

Emotionally, sunstone can lift melancholy moods and is effective for seasonal affective disorder (SAD). It encourages enthusiasm and lightens the darkness of winter.

When placed upon the Solar Plexus chakra which it aligns most strongly with, sunstone can extract heavy or repressed emotions and transmute them. It is helpful to help you move forward when you feel blocked on life's path, encouraging exploration of your possibilities and aiding spiritual expansion. It can remove the feeling of being limited in personal power or potential, opening you up to new options.

Overall, sunstone stimulates self-healing powers, inspires optimism and harmonises all the organs and energy centres. Interestingly, and as its name suggests, sunstone is particularly useful when used in the Sun.

★ TANZANITE ★

Main Spiritual & Metaphysical Qualities ★ Transformative; assists with the expansion process; transmutes karmic wounds & spiritual dis-ease; lifts depression; raises the body's wellbeing.

Astrological Affinities ★ Sagittarius, Capricorn

Magical Tips ★ Connected with the Soul Star (above the head) chakra, tanzanite helps one to speak from and adhere to the heart's truth, with all the resourcefulness and eloquence the mind can conjure. By activating our psychic abilities and raising our vibratory rate, tanzanite facilitates communication with the spiritual realms, enabling us to link with angelic beings, ascended masters, guides and other spiritual beings from other dimensions. In addition, tanzanite opens us up to 'receive' from these other worlds. With this stone's assistance, you can even access the Akashic Record for your soul.

Vibration ★ High

A member of the zoisite family, tanzanite is a mineral with a hardness of 6.5 to 7, whose colours range from blue to blue-violet, although some crystals are golden to brownish yellow (when heated to around 900 degrees Fahrenheit, the yellow-toned types turn to blue or blue-violet). Sometimes referred to by scientists as blue zoisite, tanzanite is an extraordinary purple-blue gem with violet lights flashing from its depths.

Tanzanite was first discovered as recently as 1967 in Tanzania, Africa, from where it derives its name, and was introduced by Tiffany and Co. in New York.

Tanzanite has an affinity for the Throat, Third Eye and Crown chakras, and as such is a crystal which effectively links the mind and heart; tanzanite is used to integrate the energies of both, reminding one to stay centered in the heart's wisdom while evaluating the ideas of the mind, often opening a cascade of thoughts and insights while at the same time keeping one calmly anchored.

This is a stone of transformation that dissolves old patterns of disease and karma, helping us to move forward with renewed optimism and inspiration.

Tanzanite helps us to connect to our inner source of knowledge and the Akashic realm, and improves our overall mediumship abilities. A spirit-enhancing stone, it enhances healing at all levels, as well as protecting those who are doing the healing, and gives us a sense of direction as well as allowing us to manifest our powers for the highest good.

In essence, this enchanting gem can be a teacher and healer to those who desire ascension into higher levels of awareness. It may, however, be too strong for sensitive people, as it generates a rapid psychic response that can overwhelm the mind. For this reason, it can be used with smoky quartz or hematite at your feet to help re-balance you and keep you grounded.

★ TIGER'S EYE ★

Main Spiritual & Metaphysical Qualities ★ Aids courage; protective; instils integrity & the proper use of power; promotes intuition & positive thoughts; restores balance of yin & yang energies; enhances self-confidence; grounding & affirming; assists with flexibility; alleviates depression & seasonal affective disorder (SAD).

Astrological Affinities ★ The Sun, Mercury, Gemini, Leo, Capricorn

Magical Tips ★ The commonly known yellow-brown shaded tiger's eye was considered Solar and was especially sacred to the Egyptian Sun god Ra. Its Solar associations also gave it a reputation for attracting wealth, abundance and luck. Place it around your home to attract riches and good health. Added to a charm bag, the crystal becomes a good focus for attracting prosperity and good fortune. When used in combination with spells and magic, it can help you focus more clearly on what you really want, making manifestation easier.

Vibration ★ Earthy & High

Resembling the gleaming eye of a tiger in the night, this stone has a golden streak of light which stretches full width across its polished surface, giving it an enchanting shifting lustre. A popular semi-precious member of the quartz family, its shimmering gleam effect takes its name from the beautiful chatoyant (cat's eye) effect caused by refraction of light from fibres in the crystal. Depending on the colour of this stone, it can be named after other animals also - such as hawk's eye, cat's eye, falcon's eye, ox's eye or bull's eye.

A beautiful combination of yellow-brown and chocolate-brown, tiger's eye presents pale, parallel silk-like ribbons of colour alongside deeper-hued velvety bands, transforming its colour order with each movement.

A stone from ancient times, tiger's eye has been revered for millennia all over the world for its protective and healing powers.

Tiger's eye has a particular affinity for the Solar Plexus chakra and its gold and brown colours bring together the energies of heaven and Earth, enabling us to lift our vibrations while at the same time feeling grounded, centered and stable.

The ancient belief that tiger's eye enabled one to see through things, meant that it has long been used for psychic work. A piece of tiger's eye held to the Third Eye chakra before any divination practices such as reading the Tarot, runes or scrying, is said to aid visualisation and help bring sharper images into focus. It is also thought to give clear form to dreams, desires and aspirations.

Tiger's eye is an excellent protective stone and has a positive strengthening effect on the aura when worn or carried. As a protector, it dispels fear and anxiety, and has the ability to imbue us with willpower, purpose, courage and self-confidence. If you wish to test a creative talent in public or to sell your gifts in the marketplace, tiger's eye will help you overcome a fear of failure and help you to shine! It also encourages mental clarity, allowing us to see a problem objectively, unclouded by emotions or judgement; it may therefore be used when our ideas are confused, helping us to see our goals clearly and to make the right decisions. Further, it differentiates between wishful thinking about what we *want* and what we truly *need*. Tiger's eye softens stubbornness, allowing us to see our true needs, free from our self-imposed, idealistic or rigid mental stances and attitudes stemming from unrealistic desires for perfection.

Psychologically, tiger's eye balances mood swings, as well as our yin-yang energies, and releases tension. Tiger's eye is indeed a mood-enhancer which heals issues around self-worth, depression, pride, wilfulness, self-criticism, and blocked creativity. It aids in recognising one's talents and abilities, increasing our personal power. But this is no heavy power, for truly enlightened souls are joyful, light and playful. Tiger's eye will teach you the right use of your empowerment and stop you from taking your life and your life's path so seriously.

Overall, tiger's eye provides a solid foundation for spiritual expansion. Helping us to overcome obstacles, this magical gem is one of pure bravery and is an eliminator of doubt, empowering us to fulfil our life's work without the fear of failure holding us back.

Red Tiger's Eye ★ Thought to enhance physical vitality, this stone can help create healthy patterns in exercise and eating habits. It is grounding and encourages a practical and optimistic outlook. It is used to help the wearer feel energetic, vibrantly healthy, enthusiastic, and passionate. It calms irritability and anger, especially in males. Associated with the strength and courage of the Bull or Ox, it is an antidote to anger and a fierce defence worn around the neck against any kind of bullying. For any urgent need, light a red candle and surround it with eight small red tiger's eye crystals. Drip a tiny amount of wax on each stone and when the candle had burned completely down, carry the eight crystals in a red bag with you until your desire is fulfilled.

★ TOPAZ ★

Main Spiritual & Metaphysical Qualities ★ Strengthens creativity & self-esteem; boosts confidence & positivity; eases depression; enhances imagination; energises & tones; relaxes; encourages inspiration; alleviates exhaustion; allows you to live your own truth.

Astrological Affinities ★ The Sun, Jupiter, Aries, Gemini, Leo, Scorpio, Sagittarius

Magical Tips ★ African tribal people use topaz in their ceremonies to communicate with the spirit world and to attract and manifest both wealth and health. Overall, it is an excellent stone to use for attraction and desire-drawing purposes, attracting people to you on friendship, love and business levels, and magnetising your desires as long as they are for the greater good. This stone's vibrant energy brings abundance, generosity, joy, success and good fortune, and is particularly supportive for affirmations and manifestation. As it enhances creativity, understanding and self-expression, topaz defines the essence of a true magic-worker; one who is courageous, a visionary, and filled with hope, inspiration and purpose.

Vibration ★ Earthy to High

Topaz comes from the Sanskrit word for 'fire' and has been used since ancient times. Ancient Egyptians believed it carried the golden rays of the Sun god Ra, making it a particularly significant symbol of power and protection. Usually orange-yellow or yellow-green in colour, topaz can also be found in blue, green, red, pink, yellow or colourless.

Topaz brings an energy of playfulness, lightheartedness and joy into your life, and its luminous, sparkling array of colours (light blue, green, yellow, pink) resonate with the seasons of spring and summer, times of rejuvenation, fun, renewal and hope. Topaz can be used any time you need to make a fresh start, as it will give you the energy and clarity to make a smooth and happy transition.

Aligned with the planet Jupiter, which is the planet of spiritual mastery and expansion, it strengthens and aligns the will, recharges the physical body, and promotes perception and discrimination, as well as optimism and cheerfulness.

It is believed that topaz originates from an island in the Red Sea off the coast of Egypt, which, according to legend, was plunged into thick fog day and night and solely inhabited by snakes. This island, known today as the Isle of St John, was infested with these snakes who were the guardians of the topaz. According to the legend, the flashes of these stones sparkling in the night gave a supernatural glow to the foggy island, and this famous luminosity which defied the dark forces of the night made the topaz gem a symbol of honesty, faith, purity, loyalty and righteousness.

A traditional stone of protection, topaz has long been believed to protect its wearer from harm. In ancient times amulets were made from topaz to protect the wearer from evil spirits or misfortunes, and legend had it that it changed colour to warn the wearer of imminent danger. The ancients also believed in its ability to arouse passions and intense feelings, to inspire enthusiasm and commitment, to regenerate the body, and to uncover acts of treachery and deceit, hence its connection and resonance with the zodiac sign of Scorpio also.

Topaz has the power to magnetise prosperity, honour, glory and recognition of your worth. An empathetic stone that directs energy to where it is needed most, it soothes, heals, recharges, stimulates, remotivates, and aligns the meridians of the body. As well as promoting forgiveness and truth, it helps shed light upon one's path, tap into inner resources, and highlight goals. Eliminating doubt and uncertainty, topaz also encourages a sense of trust in the Universe, that enables you to simply *be* rather than *do*.

This is an envisioning stone and helps you see the core of any issue. It has the capacity to facilitate seeing both the bigger picture and the minute detail, recognising how they interrelate. Excellent for cleansing the aura and for inducing relaxation, topaz (particularly golden, or imperial, topaz) acts like a battery and recharges spiritually and psychically, strengthening one's faith and optimism, reminding you of your Divine origins.

With an affinity for the Sacral and Solar Plexus chakras, topaz encourages one to be benevolent in outlook and helps to promote a more selfless approach to life and be more considerate of the needs of others. It helps you discover your own inner wisdom and riches as well, making you feel confident and philanthropic and compelled to spread the good fortune and sunshine all around. As it can also reduce stress levels, it is a very useful stone for people involved in the caring professions or other stressful jobs. Encouraging relaxation and serenity, it is good for restoring calm and helping the mind to unknot itself.

With its inherent protective properties, topaz is effective in healing addictions and aiding detoxification - indeed, wearing a topaz crystal can give the immune system a boost and encourage it to cope with the challenges of withdrawal. A piece of topaz can also be worn or carried when it feels like one's willpower is wavering in any situation.

An unusual characteristic of topaz is its apparent ability to put its wearer in touch with life in other parts of the galaxy; it certainly can't hurt to try!

★ TOURMALINE ★

Main Spiritual & Metaphysical Qualities ★ Strengthening; stimulating; helps one to make decisions; overall healing.

Astrological Affinities ★ Taurus, Cancer, Scorpio, Capricorn, Pisces, Venus, Water Element

Tourmaline is a very powerful stone that recharges the body: it cleanses, purifies, and transforms dense energy into a lighter vibration, and can be worn when strength or stimulation are needed.

Pink tourmaline brings healing in the form of Love, green tourmaline is restorative, and both colours worn together bring more balance in this area. When both occur combined, the resulting gem is referred to as watermelon tourmaline.

Tourmaline can be placed on the body for general healing, but it is a complex stone - both in the aspect of its crystalline structure and its mineral composition - and because of this complexity, it can draw even more complexity. Because of this power, it causes an extra charge to be created in it that necessitates the wearer to be cautious of its force and is therefore not recommended for everyday use or wear. Tourmaline is a vital stone that definitely has its place, however.

Excellent for balancing and connecting the chakras, at a physical level this gem balances the meridians, and attracts inspiration, tolerance and compassion. Tourmaline is a potent mental healer and transmutes negative thought patterns into positive ones. As it is a high energy stone, it can boost vitality and uplift the spirits.

The tourmaline's unique positive and negative electrical properties gave it its early name of the 'the mineral magnet' *; warmth also activates it, and it has long been associated with fire, electricity and overall magnetism.

Coming in a wide variety of tints, no other family of gemstones has the richness in colour variation of the tourmaline, and within most tourmalines, rainbows abound **. It is also regarded as the 'master physician' of the mineral world, with remarkable properties and a harlequin personality. Its myriad hues are the result of the contributions made by each single original crystal in this striking stone's composition.

Strongly protective, tourmaline instils patience and teaches tact and diplomacy. It helps one to find the joy in situations, promotes inner security, alleviates depression and fear, and facilitates deeper understanding of situations.

* In times past tourmaline was classed as a mineral magnet rather than as a gem. The reason for this was its unique electrical energies which cause it, when rubbed or heated, to produce in each of its crystals a positive charge at one end and a negative charge at the other. Tourmaline is pyroelectric, developing an electrical charge when heated (making it ideal for use in thermometers). For this reason, rather than encasing this gem in another metal, for example gold, it is better to use an open claw setting which allows the electrical properties of this mineral 'magician' to act without obstruction.

** Egyptian legend tells how tourmaline made its journey from the centre of the Earth and passed over a rainbow, taking with it all the colours as its own.

★ TOURMALINE ~ BLACK ★

The Stone of Spiritual Protection

> *This black thing, one of the prettiest of the very few pretty black things in the world, is called Tourmaline.*

Ruskin

Main Spiritual & Metaphysical Qualities ★ Protective; grounding; purifying; fortifying; protects all chakras & seals the aura; supports acting & thinking positively; protects against electromagnetic & geopathic stress.

Astrological Affinities ★ Scorpio, Capricorn, Saturn

Magical Tips ★ A tool of the true spiritual alchemist, black tourmaline's purifying, protective, grounding and cleansing properties are its most crucial functions. Black tourmaline is one of the most powerful stones to ground, strengthen, purify and solidify our potential. It is most effective when cleansed in the Sun, as it is piezoelectric and pyroelectric, generating electricity through heat or pressure.

Vibration ★ Earthy

Also known as 'schorl', black tourmaline protects the body against electromagnetic stress, negativity, and psychic attack. Though less 'colourful' than other varieties, black tourmaline is one of the most popular stones used for spiritual purposes. Most black tourmaline contains iron, making it a powerfully protective stone. Effective for sensitive people who are affected by electromagnetic or geopathic toxicity, it draws the stress through your feet and transmutes it into potent Earth-healing energy.

Associated with the Earth element and Base Chakra, black tourmaline's key words are grounding, purification, and protection; indeed, it is ideal for shielding the aura from discordant psychic energies. Meditating with or carrying one of these stones can keep the auric field clear of imbalance, even in the presence of destructive forces.

Providing access to high levels of spiritual refinement, it can serve to elevate one's awareness and consciousness. This crystal is also recommended for ridding oneself of negative thoughts, anger, anxieties, and self-defeating beliefs such as unworthiness.

★ TOURMALINE ~ WATERMELON ★

Astrological Affinities ★ Aries, Cancer, Leo, Taurus, Libra, Venus

Magical Tips ★ Like all tourmalines, this stone contains unique positive and negative electrical properties which earned it its early name of the 'the mineral magnet' * (see under 'Tourmaline'); warmth also activates it, and it has long been associated with fire, electricity and magnetism.

Watermelon tourmaline, combining pink and green colourings, is a powerful 'super-activator' of the Heart chakra, linking it to the higher self and fostering love, tenderness, healing and friendship. Watermelon tourmaline, when cut across its width, will show a pink centre surrounded by a green border, resembling a slice of watermelon, hence its name.

Watermelon tourmaline in particular is good for easing distress and inducing relaxation. It is strongly protective, instils patience, and teaches tact and diplomacy. It helps one to find the joy in all circumstances, promotes inner security, alleviates depression and fear, and facilitates the understanding of situations.

This attractive stone resonates deeply with the Heart chakra, and benefits relationships. It is an excellent tonic for all love situations, healing emotional dysfunction and releasing old pain.

★ TURQUOISE ★

The Good Fortune Stone

Main Spiritual & Metaphysical Qualities ★ Attracts good fortune; purifies; enhances luck; emotionally healing; bringer of peace; dispels negative belief patterns; releases inhibitions to enable fuller expression.

Astrological Affinities ★ Leo, Scorpio, Sagittarius, Capricorn, Aquarius, Pisces, Uranus, Air Element

Magical Tips ★ Turquoise is regarded as a lucky stone, bringing protection and healing to the wearer. Worn as jewellery or carried in a pouch, turquoise is believed to absorb the essence of its owner, and is a talisman for immense good luck, money, success, fame, ambition fulfilment, and creativity. The ultimate prosperity and luck-bringer, turquoise can be kept in the centre of a pattern of blue and green crystals to attract good fortune, and also the health to enjoy it. Some superstitions around it are that it brings good luck on a Saturday, but to bring good luck, it should be given as a gift, not bought by the self. An old Arabian spell for improving your fortunes which draws on the Jupiterian aspect of turquoise, is to place one of these gems close to a window at the time of a New Moon and gaze steadily on the stone and concentrate on your desire, then recite a simple statement of your wishes to the crystal, repeating it three times.

Vibration ★ High

Turquoise has been around since the dawn of civilisation itself. It gets its name from the word *'Turkish'*, because it was such an integral part of trade in ancient European markets, where it was known as the 'Turkish Stone'.

A very ancient and powerful stone, found mainly in Persia, where it is found in veins in rock, turquoise symbolises prosperity, strength, wisdom, justice, fairness, nobility and friendship.

Magical attributes of this brilliant blue or green-blue stone are protection from the evil eye and dark forces and attracting good fortune. It is also known as the 'horseman's stone' due to the belief that it protected riders from falls. This also explains its connection to the zodiac sign Sagittarius (the centaur); it is one of the birthstones of that sign.

Turquoise is also known as the Stone of Venus, and its great quality lies in its ability to draw to itself any situation of conflict, its inner light acting as a barrier between its wearer and any negative thought patterns or harmful situations. For this reason, the ancients termed it The Celestial Stone.

Carrying a soothing blue ray, turquoise is a purification stone, dispelling negative energy and clearing electromagnetic 'smog', providing protection against pollutants and toxins within the environment.

Empathetic and balancing, turquoise balances and aligns all the chakras with the subtle bodies. In fact, it has an unusually high vibration and can thus offer profound overall healing support. Being of a blue hue, it resonates most deeply with the Throat chakra, facilitating truth, communication and expression. Used on this energy centre, it releases old beliefs and inhibitions, allowing the soul to express itself once more. Turquoise instils inner calm while remaining alert, assists in creative problem-solving, and aids creativity.

Turquoise was revered by the ancient Egyptians and favoured by the Native Americans as a travelling stone and to connect with the sky spirit Father Sky, to ask him to bring rain to increase crop yields and thereby increase prosperity. It is said to connect one with the Heavens, while healing the physical body here on Earth. Indeed, without possession of a turquoise, no medicine man could command the honour, respect and veneration his position demanded; nor would the spear or arrow of the hunter fly true to its target.

Turquoise is a symbol of generosity, sincerity and affection and it is believed to preserve friendships and make friends of enemies.

Turquoise is a most efficient healer, providing physical and spiritual solace and wellbeing. As a protective amulet, it is believed to fade or change colour to warn of infidelity, danger or illness. Placed on the Third Eye, turquoise can promote spiritual attunement, communication with higher realms, and enhance intuition and meditation.

Psychologically, turquoise is a strengthening stone and dissolves unhelpful attitudes, mood swings and self-sabotage. It even has the power to prevent panic attacks and aids recovery after a nervous breakdown.

Turquoise is said to stimulate romantic love and has the power to manifest abundance in one's experience. It soothes the emotions and clears the way to enable you to go with the flow, to express and accept who you really are and to find your perfect life path with courage, conviction and fortitude. It encourages self-compassion and shields your aura from the negative influences or emotions of others, helping you to recognise any 'dramas' you may be caught up in that are blocking your progress or true individuality.

This enchanting bright blue stone truly is one of the most ancient and long-used of all the gems, and as such, it carries the wisdom of the ages.

★ UKANITE ★

Main Spiritual & Metaphysical Qualities ★ Stabilises the emotions; calms anxiety; helps us grow as individuals; aids spiritual renewal.

Astrological Affinities ★ Taurus, Libra, Scorpio, Venus

Ukanite is a metamorphic rock, an altered form of granite. Mottled pink and green, this stone takes its name from the Unaka Range of mountains in North Carolina, where it was discovered and is still extracted. In the Unakas, it occurs in extensive rocky masses and can be extracted in great blocks.

This green rock with red veins is believed to possess virtues that aid emotional balance and the steady release of long-repressed feelings.

Ukanite resonates with the Sacral, Solar Plexus and Heart chakras, balancing both and enhancing feelings of confidence, security, self-esteem, self-worth, and accepting love and nurturance from others.

Strengthening the Solar Plexus chakra, it heightens your personal power and encourages you to be more forthright about your needs and desires, and to forge ahead more confidently to get what you want in life. It transmutes feelings of worthlessness to worthiness, self-doubt to confidence, and promotes belief in your powers and abilities.

Ukanite is a stone of transformation from negativity to positivity, promoting a sense of oneness with your Self. It promotes spiritual transmutation and rebirth, allowing you to step away from self-destructive behaviour patterns that prevent you living in peace, and in the same way is considered effective for combating depressive and melancholic moods, as its vibrations are considered to be both energising and calming, encouraging a sense of wellbeing and a more optimistic outlook.

Used alongside other crystals, ukanite is said to strengthen one's powers of visualisation.

★ VANADINITE ★

Astrological Affinities ★ Saturn, Capricorn, Earth Element

Magical Tips ★ Vanadinite can help to curb overspending and when placed in the wealth corner of your home or in your purse, it is believed to help you retain your money.

Belonging to the lead family, and rich in vanadium, a grey metallic element used for strengthening steel, vanadinite is comprised of out-of-the-ordinary, complex chemicals. Dazzlingly beautiful and tougher than steel, vanadinite crystals usually grow on dark, worn-looking rock, generously filling crevices and coating the outside with smaller, lighter coloured sunset-toned crystals.

Vanadinite has a strong connection with the Earth chakra, which sits in the Earth body beneath the feet. It is therefore a useful crystal for people who have problems accepting their physicality, as it grounds the soul into the physical body and helps it to feel comfortable in the Earthly realm.

Mentally, vanadinite fills the gap between the intellect and thought, allowing insight and rational thought to combine in an inner voice of inspired guidance. It also assists in defining and pursuing one's goals by shutting out unwanted mind clutter and inducing a state of 'no mind' so that one can be more focused on visions and journeying.

Psychologically vanadinite helps to facilitate deep inner peace by eliminating mental turmoil, clearing the mind and opening up an internal channel within the body to receive a flow of Universal energy.

★ ZIRCON ★

Astrological Affinities ★ The Sun, Jupiter, Aries, Sagittarius, Capricorn

Magical Tips ★ The positive properties of zircon are enhanced by the Sun, so charging this stone in pure sunlight can be an effective way of increasing its powers.

Zircon takes its name from the Persian word 'zargun' meaning 'golden' or 'all shades of yellow' and has long been used as an amulet and talisman. This many-coloured, transparent gem should never be underestimated either as a jewel or as a holistic healing tool.

Thought by the Ancient Greeks to strengthen the mind and bring joy to the heart, zircon once took precedence over almost all gemstones on account of its lustre and beautiful reflection of light. It comes in varieties from colourless to shades of yellow, light green and brown (also called jacinth, hyacinth and malacon), and blue and red (heat-treated only).

Red zircon can be used as a love charm and to increase personal charisma and imparts a sense of personal blessings after misfortunes. Also known as jacinth or hyacinth, red zircon can be used on both the Base and Heart chakras to great beneficial effect. In any shade, its brilliance is often equal to that of diamond. Although similar to the diamond in its lustre and light, the zircon is less authoritarian in character but still firm in its direct positive actions on psychological, spiritual and mental states of being.

Zircon holds within itself the essence of the Sun and Jupiter, which carry the energy of existence and the life-force. The overriding characteristic of this crystal is its vitality, which acts with effectiveness on both physical and mental disorders. On the spiritual plane, it promotes self-development and facilitates the expansion of the higher mind.

In ancient times, zircon was regarded as a mind tonic that prevented thoughts from straying and maintained a person's focus. It can therefore be used to boost concentration during meditation and can aid chakra work and other modes of spiritual healing. Zircon is thought to contain 'decisive' powers and is a useful stone to use when wishing to take control of a situation and overcome indecision.

Zircon strengthens one's resolve and if you are at a low ebb, it picks you up, energises you, improves your outlook, and re-attunes you to your outer environment.

An uplifting stone, zircon can help you find your inner strength, lift melancholy, dissolve your fear of failure, and tap into your potential.

★ ZOISITE ★

Astrological Affinities ★ Gemini

Zoisite comes in many different colours, including white, brown, yellow, blue, red, green, pink, lavender blue, and colourless. In commercial outlets, it is often sold with ruby in it, as a variety called ruby zoisite, the presence of ruby increasing its potency.

Zoisite transmutes negative energies into positive ones and helps you connect to the spiritual realms. Mentally, zoisite aids in realising your own ideas and developing your true Self rather than being influenced by others or trying too hard to conform. It dispels lethargy and brings repressed feelings to the surface so they can be expressed.

An essentially creative stone, zoisite can transform destructive urges into constructive ones, and helps keep the mind on track. Overall, zoisite is said to encourage creativity and vitality, and put you in touch with what you really enjoy and wish to be doing.

As zoisite is generally a slow-acting stone, for best results it should be worn over long periods of time.

★ ZOISITE ~ RUBY ★

Main Spiritual & Metaphysical Qualities ★ Activates soul memories; attracts new passion into your life; brings emotional blockages to the surface for transmutation; promotes compassion & care for others; encourages positive thinking & living with passion; alleviates grief if worn over the heart; brings spiritual comfort & release.

Astrological Affinities ★ Taurus, Gemini, Libra

Magical Tips ★ Worn over your heart, ruby zoisite can attract love and passion into your experience.

Vibration ★ Earthy & High

Ruby in zoisite, also called anyolite, is a marriage of passion and patience, between the properties of fiery ruby and earthy zoisite, containing small crystals of ruby which have become embedded within the zoisite stone.

Ruby in zoisite is said to enhance fertility, increase vigour, and help overcome laziness. It stimulates psychic abilities when placed on the Crown chakra, amplifying spirituality and engaging the body's own energy field.

Ruby in zoisite transmutes negative energy into the positive, being a spiritual comforter particularly helpful for preventing mood swings, overreactions and periods of grieving.

This unique and delightful green stone with its characteristic red inclusions carries the pink ray and the green ray, lending it a spiritual affinity with the Heart chakra. As such, it opens the heart to new possibilities and opportunities.

FINAL WORD

I sincerely hope this book has opened up new gateways of knowledge, information, inspiration and magic for you. Crystals, as well as writing and astrology, are one of my life's greatest passions and I relish sharing my insight and love of these pure mineral light-forms with others.

Since beginning this book around four years ago, I have experienced many alchemical transformations as a direct result of working with these delightful little packages of concretised light. I have worked with a vast array of semi-precious and precious gems and still continue to add to my collection almost daily (raw emerald chunks are surprisingly affordable and no less powerful than their expensive embedded-in-jewellery counterparts! I am still on a quest to find diamond that doesn't cost a fortune).

I wish you the same, that you may be enchanted, moved and utterly transformed by the pure beauty and magic that crystals invariably impart to those who understand their language.

You may seek crystals, or they may seek you - often both will occur simultaneously; above and beyond all other considerations, if a stone particularly resonates and speaks to you, it is meant to be yours. Whichever crystals you have the privilege of keeping company with, you can indeed forge a powerful partnership for life with these beautiful miracles of nature.

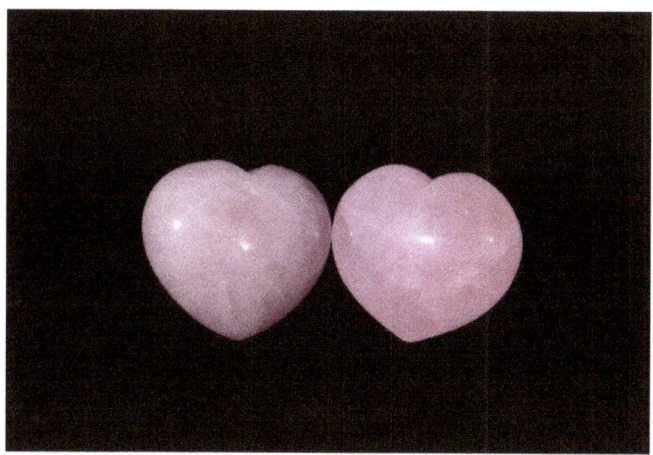

ABOUT THE AUTHOR

Lani Sharp is a crystal lover, author, astrologer, Tarot reader, free spirit, believer, dreamer & gypsy at heart, whose foray into the world of gemstones began one day in her early twenties in a small village town in Australia's northern New South Wales region, at a mystical place called *The Crystal Castle*. While there, she undertook a life-changing experiment, during which as soon as she felt the crystal's special energy permeating her body and spirit, she knew there was no turning back - and from that day onwards, crystals and gems have spoken to the depths of her soul. She loves to awaken others' interest in the topic too and hopes to provide some guidance and insights into the amazing and infinite world of minerals, gems and fossilised wonders, some forever frozen in time, but ever-evolving and giving of their powers eternally. Lani is an accredited member of the World Metaphysical Association and the Australian Astrologers Federation. She can be contacted at astrologymagick@gmail.com or via her Facebook pages *Lani Sharp Author* & *Astrology Magic*. You can also follow her on Instagram at *lani_sharp_author*.

☆   ☆   ☆

Also by Lani Sharp

Lucky Astrology ~ 12 Book Series ~ White Light Publishing

The Tarot: An Astrological Journey Through the Major Arcana ~ White Light Publishing

Divine Zodiac Messages ~ White Light Publishing

Co-Author / Contributing Author to:

Writing: The Powerful Healer ~ White Light Publishing

The Book of Inspiration For Women by Women ~ Busybird Publishing

Journey of a Lightworker ~ White Light Publishing

www.ingramcontent.com/pod-product-compliance
Lightning Source LLC
Chambersburg PA
CBHW062057290426
44110CB00022B/2625